PENGUIN
STUDENTS' GRAMMAR

RENÉ BOSEWITZ

Penguin Books

Penguin Books Ltd, Harmondsworth, Middlesex, England
Viking Penguin Inc., 40 West 23rd Street, New York, New York
10010, U.S.A.
Penguin Books Australia Ltd, Ringwood, Victoria, Australia
Penguin Books Canada Ltd, 2801 John Street, Markham, Ontario,
Canada L3R 1B4
Penguin Books (N.Z.) Ltd, 182–190 Wairau Road, Auckland 10, New
Zealand

First published 1987

Made and printed in Great Britain by
Hazell Watson & Viney Limited,
Member of the BPCC Group,
Aylesbury, Bucks

Designed by Jacky Wedgwood

Illustrated by Sean MacGarry

CONTENTS

INTRODUCTION

This book has been written to help learners of English to help themselves. It is intended for the student of English who has a basic knowledge of the language but still has problems in understanding its mechanics. This book (1) gives an overview of the main structures of English in context, (2) isolates the form of the individual structures, and (3) explains when and how they are used in communication. It puts into perspective the grammar necessary to take the Elementary learner through to an Intermediate/Advanced level for an examination like, for example, the Cambridge First Certificate.

It can be used both individually and in the classroom.

The book is organized in a traditional manner in order to give the reader a clear point of reference; the chapter headings show the reader where to look for Nouns, Adjectives, Modal Verbs, etc. Since many students have met these terms before, it was considered useful to build around them, though explanations are expressed in simple English rather than in grammar terminology.

In the past, many different terms have been used to describe English grammar. This has often caused confusion. These terms are defined within the text and they, and alternatives to them, as well as specific points, can be found by reference to the index at the back of the book. The book is cross-referenced throughout, so that more information about each point can easily be found. Illustrations and diagrams further clarify some points.

Although it describes the forms and structures of English, the book emphasizes the context and situations in which we use them. It combines, therefore, information about the communicative use of a grammar item and a description of its form.

The presentation of each item follows the same pattern, and the reader should soon become familiar with it:

Text/Dialogue	Form	Communicative use	Extra information	Bird's eye box
Grammar item presented in context	Form of item given without context	Way or ways in which item used, with examples	Exceptions in use and additional information about item	Overview of uses of item for revision

The aim in writing a practical grammar to an Intermediate/Advanced level was to present the learner with a skeleton framework on which to build later. To this end, therefore, only the more important rules have been selected.

There are always exceptions to the general rules of grammar in a language. In the author's experience the foreign learner is often dismayed and frustrated by an abundance of these exceptions. Thus this grammar is concerned with exposing the reader to the main points in the language and explaining what we want to communicate when we use them.

In addition, a real effort has been made to keep the explanations and extra information as simple as possible for the foreign learner who may not be completely clear about the form and use of a particular structure.

The texts and dialogues, which form the basis of the presentation of the items, cover a wide range of situations. The learner's attention is drawn to differences between spoken and written, formal and informal forms in English.

It is hoped this book will help the learner to see grammar as an integral part of the full communication process and not as a separate and disconnected study.

René Bosewitz
Heidelberg, 1987

1 NUMERALS

CONTENTS		page

1.1 Cardinal numbers

SHOP MANAGER: Today we're going to make a list of some of the goods in the shop. Jenny, could you begin with the things on your shelf?

ten, five, fifteen, twenty-five

JENNY: Well, I've got **ten** packets of soap powder, **five** bars of soap, **fifteen** bottles of shampoo and **twenty-five** tubes of toothpaste.

SHOP MANAGER: Bob, have you counted your things yet?

thirty, twenty-two

BOB: Yes, I've got **thirty** bags of sugar, **twenty-two** packets of tea . . .

SHOP MANAGER: All right, all right. Just write everything down. Then we'll go to the store-room and count the things there.

--- form ---

0*	nought, nil,	11	eleven	22	twenty-two
	zero, 0, /əʊ/	12	twelve	23	twenty-three
1	one	13	thirteen	24	twenty-four
2	two	14	fourteen	25	twenty-five
3	three	15	fifteen	30	thirty
4	four	16	sixteen	40	forty
5	five	17	seventeen	50	fifty
6	six	18	eighteen	60	sixty
7	seven	19	nineteen	70	seventy
8	eight	20	twenty	80	eighty
9	nine	21	twenty-one	90	ninety
10	ten				

100	a/one hundred	102	a/one hundred and two
101	a/one hundred and one	120	a/one hundred and twenty

130	a/one hundred	1000	a/one thousand
	and thirty	1003	a/one thousand and three
200	two hundred	1004	a/one thousand and four
300	three hundred	2000	two thousand
400	four hundred		
500	five hundred	100,000	a/one hundred thousand
		1,000,000	a/one million

* We usually pronounce 0 as 'owe': for example, when giving telephone and bus numbers.

USE

Counting things – 1, 2, 3,   one, two, three

We use CARDINAL NUMBERS when we want to count things or people.

We can say how many things there are in a situation by putting a number in front of the NOUN (the name of a thing – see Chapter 2) to which they refer:

There are **365** (three hundred and sixty-five) **days** in a year.

She has **£3500** (three thousand five hundred **pounds**) in the bank.

We often ask the question **how many?** when we want to know the number of people or things in a situation:

MIKE: **How many** windows are there in your house, Paul?
PAUL: There are **four**.

Hyphens in numbers – twenty-one, fifty-five, ninety-nine

When we write numbers like the following as words we put a HYPHEN (⁃) (24.12) between the two parts:

> ↓ ↓ ↓
> 22, 23, 24, etc. → twenty-two, twenty-three, twenty-four, etc.
> 32, 33, 34, etc. → thirty-two, thirty-three, thirty-four, etc.
> 41, 44, 48, etc. → forty-one, forty-four, forty-eight, etc.

1.2 Ordinal numbers

first

fourth, second
thirty-second

third

SPORTS REPORTER: Rod Villiers is the **first** New Zealander to win this tennis competition. Last year he was placed **fourth** in the competition, **second** in his own country and **thirty-second** in the world. His tennis this year has been so entertaining that we really hope to see him back next year. And if he wins again next year it will be only the **third** time in history that a player has won the competition twice in a row.

--- **form** ---

1st	first	18th	eighteenth
2nd	second	19th	nineteenth
3rd	third	20th	twentieth
4th	fourth	21st	twenty-first
5th	fifth	22nd	twenty-second
6th	sixth	23rd	twenty-third
7th	seventh	24th	twenty-fourth
8th	eighth	30th	thirtieth
9th	ninth	40th	fortieth
10th	tenth	50th	fiftieth
11th	eleventh	90th	ninetieth
12th	twelfth	100th	the (one) hundredth
13th	thirteenth	101st	the (one) hundred
14th	fourteenth		and first
15th	fifteenth	1000th	the (one) thousandth
16th	sixteenth	1,000,000th	the (one) millionth
17th	seventeenth		

Position in a series – 1st, 2nd, 3rd   first, second, third

We use ORDINAL NUMBERS when we want to show the position of something or somebody in a series:

JOHN: You see those cars in the showroom window? Which one do you like best?

PETER: The green Fiat. It's the **second** from the right.

Dates

We use ordinal numbers in dates:

I was born on **3** April, 1949/**3rd** April, 1949/April **3**, 1949/April **3rd**, 1949. (written English)
I was born on April **the third** nineteen forty-nine/**the third** of April nineteen forty-nine. (spoken English)

Hyphens

Ordinal numbers take a hyphen in the same way as cardinal numbers (1.1):

	↓
21st	⟶ twenty-first
34th	⟶ thirty-fourth
45th	⟶ forty-fifth

9

1.3 Number of times

We use **once**, **twice**, **three times** as follows:

once = one time	I visited Greece **once**.
twice = two times	She paid the electricity bill **twice**.
three times	They went to the cinema together **three times**.

 once can mean 'one time'. It can also refer to some time in the past – we do not know when:

We **once** hoped to buy a boat, but now it's impossible.

I **once** wanted to join the army, but now I can't understand why.

Contrast

ONE TIME	SOME TIME IN THE PAST
He took time off for illness only **once**.	He **once** tried to climb Mount Everest.
or	
He only **once** took time off for illness.	

1.4 Vulgar fractions

half
fifth
three tenths
a quarter
nine tenths

The students in Dave's class in Italy had a discussion about how they had spent their money while on a course in England. One said that he had spent **half** on entertainment and a **fifth** on transport. The remaining **three tenths** had been spent on books, clothes, and phoning home. Most students had spent at least **a quarter** on entertainment and some had spent as much as **nine tenths**.

─── **form** ───

½	a/one half	⅔	two thirds
⅓	a/one third	¾	three quarters
¼	a/one quarter	⅘	four fifths
⅕	a/one fifth	1¼	one and a quarter
⅙	a/one sixth	1½	one and a half

USE

Part of a whole – ½, ⅔, ¾   half, two thirds, three quarters

We use VULGAR FRACTIONS when we want to describe something as a part of a whole:

KATHRYN: How much of that apple-juice is left?
ROY: I'm afraid only **half** of it.

They have already eaten **one third** of the cake.

1.5 Decimal fractions

USE

Part of a whole – 3.75, 7.32, 9.03   three point seven five, seven point three two, nine point o three

We can also express parts of a whole in the form of DECIMAL FRACTIONS. We separate a whole number from a fraction with a point (.). This is a form which people often use when they are talking about statistics. We pronounce each number which appears after the point separately:

VULGAR		DECIMAL	
we write	*we say*	we write	*we say*
1½	one and a half	1.5	one point five
2¼	two and a quarter	2.25	two point two five
3¾	three and three quarters	3.75	three point seven five
1¹/₂₀	one and a twentieth	1.05	one point o★ five
		★ Pronounced 'owe'/əʊ/ (1.1).	

11

1.6 Bird's eye box: Numerals

She has **two** cars.	$\longrightarrow$	cardinal number
This is her **second** car.	$\longrightarrow$	ordinal number
Man has walked on the moon **twice**.	$\longrightarrow$	number of times
Three quarters (¾) of the world are hungry.	$\longrightarrow$	vulgar fraction
The average family has **two point five** (2.5) children.	$\longrightarrow$	decimal fraction

2 NOUNS

CONTENTS

2.1 Nouns (general)

system	DAVID: I want to buy a new stereo **system**: the best
systems	**systems** come from Japan, I think.
record-players, cassette	RUDOLF: Yes, **record-players** and **cassette recorders**
recorders, prices	from Japan are top quality but they cost top **prices**,
department store	too. I think you should go to a big **department store**.
system	You might find a really cheap **system** there.
make	DAVID: Could you tell me which **make** I should look for
items	and what the individual **items** are likely to cost?

───────── **form** ─────────

definite article + noun (singular/plural)

| the | item |
| the | televisions |

indefinite article + noun (singular)

| a | system |
| an | idea |

possessive adjective + noun (singular/plural)

| my | television |
| your | mistakes |

What is a noun?

A NOUN is the name of a person, place or thing.

It can be CONCRETE (you can see or touch it):

girl   John   telephone   street   tree   bird

or it can be ABSTRACT (you cannot see or touch it):

love   time   anger   happiness   wealth

A NOUN PHRASE is a group of words including a noun but without a subject or main verb:

an old man   the shop with the red sign

USE

What do nouns do in a sentence?

We use nouns in several situations in a sentence:

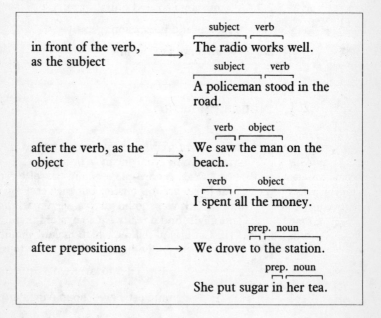

in front of the verb, as the subject	subject verb The radio works well. subject verb A policeman stood in the road.
after the verb, as the object	verb object We saw the man on the beach. verb object I spent all the money.
after prepositions	prep. noun We drove to the station. prep. noun She put sugar in her tea.

2.2 Regular plurals

things

HOTEL GUEST: Some **things** have been stolen from my room. Can you do anything about it?

HOTEL MANAGER: What has been taken?

HOTEL GUEST: I've checked very carefully and I've written it all down. The thief took two gold **watches**, all my travellers' **cheques** and credit **cards** and even my two best **suits**.

watches
cheques, cards
suits

clothes

> HOTEL MANAGER: What were the watches worth? I'll have to write it down for the police.
> HOTEL GUEST: They cost £200 each, and the **clothes** are worth £300 altogether.

---

form

noun + **s/es**

(two) ticket___s
(some) coin___s
(the) answer___s
(three) dog___s
(many) friend___s
(four) watch___es
(five) bus___es

USE

one (1) thing → two (2) things

We use the PLURAL of a noun when there is more than one of a thing or person in a situation:

JOHN: David! You look sick. How **many** glasses of milk have you drunk?

DAVID: I feel sick. In fact, I've had **five** glasses of milk.

 1 Most nouns – ___s, ___es

The most common way to make a noun plural is to add **s** to the singular:

hat → hats   friend → friends   book → books

Singular nouns which end in **o**, **ss**, **ch**, **sh**, **x** or **s** form their plural with **es**:

potato → potatoes   kiss → kisses
church → churches   wish → wishes
box → boxes   bus → buses

2 Nouns ending with y

When a noun ends with **y** preceded by a vowel (a, e, i, o, u), the plural is formed by adding **s**:

day → days   boy → boys   monkey → monkeys

When a noun ends with **y** preceded by a CONSONANT (3.6), the plural is formed by dropping **y** and adding **ies**:

baby → babies   country → countries

Pronunciation of plurals

 There are three ways of pronouncing the plural endings of nouns. It is necessary to consider the last letters of the singular form and the sound that they make.

/s/	/z/	/iz/
soups	boards	bushes
moths	knobs	losses
gates	rooms	faces
cakes	windows	hedges
	valves	watches
	pens	
	fools	
	pears	
	frogs	
	lathes	

2.3 Compound nouns

 When a noun has two or more parts, it is called a COMPOUND NOUN:

1 2	1 2	1 2 3
boy-friend	wrist-watch	mother-in-law

The plural of most compound nouns is formed by adding **s** or **es** to the final part of the word:

grown-ups   boy-friends   spoonfuls   wrist-watches

The plural of a few compound nouns is formed by adding **s** or **es** to the first part of the word:

passers-by   mothers-in-law*

*In everyday conversation 'mother-in-laws' is quite common.

2.3.1 Irregular plurals

 Some nouns have a different form in the plural:

child	→ children	mouse	→	mice
foot	→ feet	ox	→	oxen
gentleman	→ gentlemen	person	→	people
goose	→ geese	shelf	→	shelves
knife	→ knives	tooth	→	teeth
man	→ men	woman	→	women

2.3.2 Mostly a plural form

 Some nouns are usually found only in the plural:

A surroundings earnings premises* thanks goods*

B spectacles* glasses* shorts trousers jeans pyjamas braces* pants clothes

C scissors scales* shears goggles

* Note that these nouns can be used in the singular when they have other meanings.

We can describe the items in B and C as **a pair of** spectacles, **a pair of** jeans, **a pair of** goggles, etc.:

He is short-sighted. He needs to wear **a pair of** strong **glasses**.

A pair of jeans costs £15 nowadays.

When there is more than one pair we add **s**:

two pairs of glasses   **three** pairs of jeans

2.3.3 Mostly a singular form

 Some nouns are usually found only in the singular. They represent a plural idea and are all followed by a singular VERB (9.1):

advice business* expenditure homework information knowledge news progress furniture equipment †hair

* See page 18.
† Can be plural when it is used as a countable noun.

Business **was** bad before the new manager came.
This advice **was** extremely useful to me.
The news today **is** very exciting.
Some knowledge of grammar **helps** us to understand how language works.

NOTE

We can also precede these nouns with **some** (8.3) or **a lot of** (8.1):

The staff at the British Embassy gave me **some** advice about my work permit.

Last year we made **a lot of** progress but this year has not been so good.

---

* In the example on page 17, **business** means 'commerce' or 'trading'. We can use **business** in the plural to mean 'shops' or other commercial 'enterprises':

The family owns **three** small businesses.

2.3.4 Same singular and plural form

 The names of some animals have the same form in the plural as in the singular:

sheep   fish   salmon   deer

There are **sixteen sheep** in the field.

He caught **several fish** with his new fishing rod.

2.4 Nouns and possession (genitive)

Terry's house

Jim's place, Terry's

Jim's parents parents' attitude

JOHN: What time are we meeting at **Terry's house** this evening?

WILLY: Actually, the party's at **Jim's place**, not **Terry's**. And there'll be more than a hundred people there.

JOHN: Well, I hope they won't cause too much damage. **Jim's parents** are very strict about that sort of thing.

WILLY: That's right. But I think his **parents' attitude** to young people is rather unfair.

—————————— **form** ——————————

noun (singular) + **'s** + noun (singular/plural)

Terry___'s   house

John___'s   friend

my friend___'s   bicycle

noun (plural) + ' + noun (singular/plural)	
his parents_____'	house
the ladies_____'	cloakroom
the students_____'	books
the mens_____'	jeans

Whose book? ⟶ Mary's book

When we want to show that something belongs to a person we use the APOSTROPHE (') (24.11). When we want to know who something belongs to we ask a question beginning with **whose**.

QUESTION	ANSWER
Whose house is this? ⟶	This is David's house. (The house belongs to David.)
Whose car is it? ⟶	It's Mary's car. (The car belongs to Mary.)
Whose idea was that? ⟶	It was Jenny's idea. (The idea came from Jenny.)
Whose books are these? ⟶	These are the students' books. (These are the books which belong to the students.)

Notice the **books** belong to more than one student. **Students'** is the plural form. We put the apostrophe after a plural which ends in **s**:

The teachers' cars are all parked behind the school.

The new secretaries' desks are on the left of the office.

When the plural of a noun does not end in **s** we add **'s**:

children → The children's playground is near the shops.
men → The men's department is on the second floor.

2.5 Bird's eye box: Nouns

The **car** works well.	⟶ noun
There are three **cups** on the table.	⟶ regular plural
He took a **handful** of bread to feed to the birds.	⟶ compound noun
Two **men** came to the door.	⟶ irregular plural
Many **thanks** for your help.	⟶ mostly a plural form
His **progress** was slow.	⟶ mostly a singular form
David's car is a Fiat.	⟶ possession (singular)
Here are the **students'** books.	⟶ possession (plural)

3 ARTICLES

CONTENTS

3.1 Definite article (to specify)

ROY: When we arrive in York let's find a swimming pool so that we can get some exercise. It's been a long day and I'd like a swim.

the
the DAVID: Well, there's **the** Queen Street Swimming Pool in **the** centre of town.
the ROY: Is that **the** one on **the** corner opposite **the** Town Hall?
DAVID: That's it. There are several pools in York but **the**
the Queen Street one is about **the** best. **The** others are a bit too expensive.
ROY: OK. Let's go.

───── **form** ─────

the + noun singular / plural

the man	the men
the pool	the pools
the centre	the centres

USE 1

the ⟶ the specific one

We put **the** before a NOUN (see Chapter 2) when we want to show that we are talking about a specific object or objects. David says:

'There's **the** Queen Street Swimming Pool.'

He is talking about one particular swimming pool.

Look at the following:

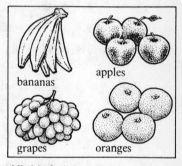

These drinks all taste good but I like **the** mineral water most of all.

All this fruit is delicious, but I like **the** oranges best.

USE 2

the ⟶ something mentioned earlier

We also use **the** to refer to a noun which we have mentioned earlier in a conversation or written in a text. David says:

'**the** Queen Street [Swimming Pool] is about **the** best.'

the refers to the noun 'Queen Street Swimming Pool', mentioned earlier in the sentence.

He bought a new **stereo system** last week. It's **the** one we looked at together in Oxford Street.

Mary is the girl for the job. **The** others [the *other* girls] need more experience.

3.2 Definite article (something unique)

the the the the the	DAD: What did you learn at school today? SON: **The** highest mountain in **the** world is in the Himalayas; **the** largest ocean is **the** Pacific; **the** largest island is Greenland; **the** largest planet is Jupiter; **the** nearest planet to **the** Earth is . . . DAD: Stop! Stop! Is that everything? SON: No. The teacher talked for over an hour. It was **the** most boring lesson this year!

USE 1

the ⟶ the only one

We use **the** in front of a noun when it refers to something unique (i.e. there is only one of its kind). Very often these nouns are geographical names or places (although we do not normally use **the** before names of countries or towns):

the sun   **the** moon   **the** universe   **the** City of London
the Pacific Ocean   **the** Hebrides   **the** West Indies
the United States of America   **the** USSR

USE 2

Superlatives

We use **the** in front of SUPERLATIVE ADJECTIVES (6.6):

It was **the best** holiday I've ever had.

3.3 the + adjective as a noun

USE

When we want to talk about a whole group of people we can use **the** in front of certain adjectives:

the poor   **the** unemployed   **the** sick   **the** old   **the** lonely

In some countries **the poor** become poorer and **the rich** become richer. In a social welfare state we must take care of **the sick** and **the lonely**.

the poor ⟶ all poor people
the sick ⟶ all sick people

3.4 No definite article (zero article)

Arthur
Saudi Arabia

Europe
Christmas

summer
spring, autumn

> BRYAN: **Arthur**, I heard that you have lost your job in **Saudi Arabia**. What happened?
> ARTHUR: Well, I didn't actually lose my job. I decided that I wanted to work in **Europe** again. I came home at **Christmas**.
> BRYAN: But I thought you were earning a lot of money in **Saudi Arabia**. You'll never get that much back here.
> ARTHUR: Yes, it's possible to earn money but the problem for a European is the climate. **Summer** is too hot and they don't really have **spring** and **autumn**.

3.4.1 No definite article (names, countries, festivals, days, etc.)

USE 1

We do not put **the** in front of the following groups of words (see also ☞ 1 and ☞ 2 below):

A

> **First names**
> Peter   John   Sheila
> Chris   Marc

B

> **Countries**
> England   Scotland
> Belgium   Singapore
> Egypt   Brazil   (see ☞ 1)

C

> **Festivals**
> Easter   Whitsun
> Christmas   Ramadan

D

> **Days and months**
> Monday   Tuesday
> Thursday   Friday
> January   February
> July   September
> December

E

> **Seasons**
> summer   winter
> spring   autumn

F

> **Meals**
> breakfast   lunch
> dinner   tea   supper
> elevenses

1 A few countries do take **the**:

the United States   **the** Soviet Union   **the** Netherlands
the United Kingdom

2 The words in groups C, D, E and F can take **the** when we are talking about a specific festival, month, day, season or meal:

Breakfast is a meal that I do not normally enjoy but **the breakfast** we ate today was extremely good.

3.4.2 No definite article (abstract nouns)

USE 2

We do not put **the** in front of ABSTRACT NOUNS (2.1) when we speak generally about them:

> life   death   space   time   love   hatred   history
> poverty   wealth   honesty   happiness

Death is **life**'s final joke!
Time seems to pass more quickly as you get older.

 We do put **the** in front of the nouns in 3.4.2 when we speak specifically:

Life can be interesting, but **the life** I led as a teenager was terrible.

3.4.3 No definite article (uncountable and plural countable nouns (specific))

(See 8.1 for COUNTABLE and UNCOUNTABLE nouns.)

USE 3

We do not put **the** in front of (singular) uncountable nouns or plural countable nouns when we speak generally:

Cows are docile creatures.
Cheese is good for you.

3.5 Bird's eye box: Definite article

That is **the** man I saw at the museum.	⟶ to specify
Men have walked on **the** moon.	⟶ for something unique
He is **the** funniest teacher.	⟶ superlatives
Spring is our most beautiful season.	⟶ no definite article before names, countries, festivals, days, months, seasons, meals, abstract nouns, uncountable and plural countable nouns

3.6 Indefinite article (general)

a a a a	JENNY: It's lovely to be here on the beach today. It's **a** wonderful place to swim, too. There's even **a** small restaurant where we can get **a** meal later on. PAT: We must be careful, though. Beach restaurants can be very expensive. JENNY: You're **a** typical accountant. You can't enjoy **a** day at the sea without thinking about how much it costs!

```
┌──────────────────── form ─────────────────────┐
│                                                │
│          a/an + noun (singular)                │
│                  │                             │
│          a       │ manager                     │
│          a       │ pound                       │
│          a       │ person                      │
│             an   │ envelope                    │
│             an   │ artist                      │
│                  │                             │
└────────────────────────────────────────────────┘
```

 We use **a** in front of a word which begins with a consonant:

```
┌────────────────────────────────────────────────┐
│  b c d f g h j k l m n p q r s t v               │
│  w x y z                                         │
└────────────────────────────────────────────────┘
```

a sister   a day   a train   a present

We use **an** in front of a noun which begins with a vowel:

```
┌─────────────────┐
│  a e i o u      │
└─────────────────┘
```

an egg   an orange   an idea

DANGER

The silent h – honest, hour

In some words we do not say the initial **h**. We put **an** in front of these words. If we say the **h** we put **a** in front.

an (h)onest man   *but* a heart
an (h)our   *but* a hero

u as a consonant

In some words the **u** at the beginning has the sound /ju/.
It is no longer a vowel but has become a consonant. We put **a** in front of these words:

a uniform   /ˈjuːnɪfɔːm/   *but* an umbrella
            (yuniform)
a union   /ˈjuːnjən/   *but* an ugly face/
            (yunion)

3.7   a/an ⟶ one person or thing (unspecified)

USE 1

We use **a/an** in front of a single countable noun when it is mentioned for the first time and refers to an unspecified person or thing:

26

a man → one man – we do not know who
a house → one house – we do not know which
He bought a car. → He bought one car – we do not know
anything special about it.

3.7.1   a/an ——→ job, religion, nationality

USE 2

We use **a/an** in front of nouns which tell us about a person's
job, religion or nationality:

He's **a/an** Protestant/engineer/Arab.
She's **a** Norwegian/nurse/Catholic.

3.7.2   Expressions of frequency and measurement

USE 3

We use **a/an** when we talk about how many times something
happens:

I buy a new car twice   **a** year.
The post arrives once   **a** week.

We also use **a/an** when we measure things (speed, cost, etc.):

The meat costs two pounds (£2)   **a**   kilogram.
This material is fifty pence (50p)   **a**   metre.
He drove at fifty miles   **an**   hour.

3.7.3   Exclamations

USE 4

a/an is used in exclamations before singular COUNTABLE
nouns (8.1):

What **a** horrible **thing** to say!   What **an** interesting **book**!
What **a** beautiful **day**!   What **a** stupid **cat**!

3.8   Bird's eye box: Indefinite article

It's **a** lovely area.	——→	one unspecified thing (also person)
She's **a** social worker.	——→	job (also religion/ nationality)
They swim once **a** week.	——→	frequency
It cost £3 **a** metre.	——→	measurement
What **an** expensive jacket!	——→	exclamations

4 PRONOUNS

CONTENTS

4.1 Personal pronouns (subject)

I, we

they, it

she

> JAMES: **I** think **we** should hold a party this evening. **We** could invite all the foreign students from the language school. **They** would certainly enjoy it. **It** would also give them a chance to improve their English.
> JOHN: Cynthia said **she**'d do the cooking.

─────── **form** ───────

pronoun (subject)   pronoun (subject)

$$\left.\begin{array}{l}\text{I} \\ \text{you} \\ \text{he} \\ \text{she} \\ \text{it}\end{array}\right\} + \text{verb (singular)} \qquad \left.\begin{array}{l}\text{we} \\ \text{you} \\ \text{they}\end{array}\right\} + \text{verb (plural)}$$

USE

We use a PERSONAL PRONOUN as the SUBJECT when we want to talk about somebody or something we have mentioned before and do not wish to repeat the noun in question:

Peter speaks English. **He** speaks it very well.
not
Peter speaks English. **Peter** speaks it very well.

Look at the following:

1	2 (verb)	
I	saw	John yesterday.
He	tells	everybody what he thinks.
They	are going	to London tomorrow.

The subject pronoun is in position 1, in front of the verb.

I	$\longrightarrow$	means the person who is speaking.
you	$\longrightarrow$	means the person or people we are speaking to (both singular *and* plural).
he	$\longrightarrow$	means we are talking about a man or boy.
she	$\longrightarrow$	means we are talking about a woman or girl.
it	$\longrightarrow$	means we are talking about an animal or thing.
we	$\longrightarrow$	means the person speaking and at least one other person.
they	$\longrightarrow$	means we are talking about more than one person or thing.

4.1.1 Personal pronouns (object)

it
me
us
you

them

> PAINTER: Well. The room is twenty metres square. I
> think we could paint **it** in two days.
> HOUSE-OWNER: Can you give **me** an estimate? What do
> you reckon it will cost **us**?
> PAINTER: I can't tell **you** until I've checked all the walls.
> I need to know what the surface is like. I expect I can
> do the job for under £150.
> HOUSE-OWNER: That's a bit expensive, isn't it? We had
> three rooms painted last year and didn't pay more than
> £90 for any of **them**.

form

pronoun (object)

$$
\text{verb} \; + \;
\left.
\begin{array}{l}
\text{me} \\
\text{you} \\
\text{him} \\
\text{her} \\
\text{it}
\end{array}
\right\}
\text{(singular)}
$$

$$
\text{verb} \; + \;
\left.
\begin{array}{l}
\text{us} \\
\text{you} \\
\text{them}
\end{array}
\right\}
\text{(plural)}
$$

USE 1

We use a PERSONAL PRONOUN as the OBJECT when we want
to talk about somebody or something we have mentioned
before and do not wish to repeat the noun in question:

I know **Mary**. I see **her** every day.
not
I know **Mary**. I see **Mary** every day.

Look at the following. The object pronoun is in position 3,
after the verb:

1	2 (verb)	3
They	saw	**me** take the money.
I	heard	**you** come home last night.
You	could give	**him** the money.
She	feeds	**them** every day.

4.1.2 Personal pronouns (after prepositions)

USE 2

We can use a personal pronoun (object) after a PREPOSITION:
(see Chapter 21):

The librarian gave the book **to him**.
He threw a stone **at her**.
We bought the presents especially **for them**.

4.1.3 Personal pronouns (after be)

USE 3

We can use a personal pronoun (object) after the VERB **be** (9.1–9.3):

JIM: Who's knocking at the door?
PETER: It's John.
JIM: It can't be **him**.

It's **me**.   It's **her**.   It's **them**.

4.2 General pronouns (one, you)

USE

When we want to talk about people in general (not specific people) we can use the GENERAL PRONOUN **one**:

One should always wait at a zebra crossing. ⎫ These mean
People should always wait at a zebra crossing. ⎭ the same.

One can also be used to replace a noun:
Give John a sweet. He's got **one**.

But **you** is much more usual and is less formal. It also means 'all people', 'everybody':

You should always be careful when **you**'re crossing the road.
You don't need a passport to go to Scotland.

4.3 Bird's eye box: Personal/general pronouns

I   you   he   she   it   we
you   they   ⟶   subject pronouns

She plays the piano.

me   you   him   her   it   us
you   them   ⟶   object pronouns

The man saw **him** in the car.

one   you

In England **you** can learn to
drive at seventeen.
                                    ⟶   general pronouns
One must learn the rules by
heart.

4.4 Possessive pronouns

JUDY: I can't wait for the summer holidays to end. The
children are so bored. They're always arguing with
each other – and with me! How are **yours**?

yours
mine
yours

TERESA: **Mine**? They're just the same! But I always
thought **yours** were rather angelic!

JUDY: Not at all! They just give that impression to
people outside the family!

yours
ours

TERESA: Well, I'm glad to hear that **yours** are not more
perfect than **ours**!

form

pronoun (subject) ⟶ possessive pronoun

I ⟶	mine	
you ⟶	yours	
he ⟶	his	(singular)
she ⟶	hers	
it ⟶	its	
we ⟶	ours	
you ⟶	yours	(plural)
they ⟶	theirs	

USE

Belonging – something belongs to us. It is ours.

We use a POSSESSIVE PRONOUN to show that something
belongs to us (see also POSSESSIVE ADJECTIVES 4.5). A
possessive pronoun does *not* stand in front of a noun. It gives
the idea very strongly that something belongs to somebody:

The idea was **mine**.   (and not another person's)

It was **yours**, wasn't it? (and not his or hers)

Contrast

POSSESSIVE ADJECTIVE		POSSESSIVE PRONOUN
A: Was that **your car** you were driving yesterday?	⟶	B: **Mine**? No, in fact it was my father's.
A. Why were you driving **his car**?	⟶	B: Well, it is **his** but he lends it to me sometimes.

32

4.5 Possessive adjectives

<table>
<tr><td>my</td><td>

At the cloakroom

GUEST 1: Excuse me. I think you've taken **my** coat by mistake.
</td></tr>
<tr><td>your, my
his, my
my</td><td>GUEST 2: Pardon. **Your** coat? No, this is definitely **my** own coat. Anyway, everybody has **his** own ticket. **My** ticket number is six and **my** coat is hanging on number six.
GUEST 1: Look! I've got number six as well.</td></tr>
<tr><td>your</td><td>GUEST 2: You haven't got number six. **Your** number is nine. You're holding it upside down!</td></tr>
</table>

form

pronoun (subject) ⟶ possessive adjective

I	⟶	my	
you	⟶	your	(singular) + noun
he	⟶	his	singular/plural
she	⟶	her	
it	⟶	its	

we	⟶	our	
you	⟶	your	(plural) + noun
they	⟶	their	singular/plural

USE

Belonging – it is our car.

When we want to show that something belongs to us we can use a POSSESSIVE ADJECTIVE. It stands in front of the noun we want to describe (see also POSSESSIVE PRONOUNS, 4.4):

JANE: Whose coat are you wearing?
MARY: It's **my** coat. (The coat belongs to me.)

Sally is very upset because **her** house burned down last night.

The students are quite happy because **their** examination results were good.

4.6 Double possessive

a . . . of hers
a . . . of his
some . . . of ours

> MRS SMITH: Mary was telling me recently that **a friend of hers** has just had an operation on his leg.
> MRS JONES: Really? My husband told me that **a** workmate **of his** was in hospital for something to do with his leg. What sort of operation was it?
> MRS SMITH: I don't know exactly. **Some** friends **of ours** who know the man well said that he had fallen down the stairs in the factory where he works.

form

article	+ noun	+ of	+ possessive pronoun
a	cousin	of	mine
the	friend	of	hers
some	money	of	ours
any	arguments	of	yours
both	children	of	theirs

USE

The form is special because it tells us that the thing which belongs to us is part of a whole or one of several and not one special one.

He is a friend **of mine**.
⟶ He is one of my friends – I have others.

Tonight I'm going to have dinner with a colleague **of mine**.
⟶ He/she is one of several colleagues.

Some money **of ours** was stolen.
⟶ But the rest of our money is safe.

4.7 Bird's eye box: Possessive pronouns/adjectives

> mine yours his hers its
> ours yours theirs ⟶ possessive pronouns
>
> The big, blue car is **theirs**.
>
> my your his her its
> our your their ⟶ possessive adjectives
>
> I believe this is **your** book.

34

> By mistake he took **a pen of mine.** ⟶ double possessive

4.8 Reciprocal pronoun (each other)

each other
each other

> *At Victoria Station*
>
> EVE: Hello Dick! I didn't expect to see you here. We haven't seen **each other** for years.
> DICK: Do we know **each other**? I'm sorry, I remember the face but I can't give it a name.
> EVE: You remember me. Eve! We went to school together.
> DICK: That's right. But you've changed so much. I didn't recognize you.
>
> ── **form** ──
>
> verb + **each other**
>
> | we saw | each other |
> | they're hitting | each other |
>
> verb + preposition + **each other**
>
> | we laughed | at | each other |
> | they pointed | at | each other |
> | you played | with | each other |

USE 1

You do it to me and I do it to you

When we want to describe two people doing something together and the action in the situation passes from one to the other we can use **each other**:

John and Claire **met each other** in the street.
⟶ John met Claire and Claire met John.

The two boxers **are hitting each other** very hard.
——→Both boxers are taking part in the action.

 After prepositions

(See Chapter 21 for PREPOSITIONS.)

They are terribly in love **with each other**.
John and Jim spoke **to each other**.

☞ **one another**

They waited for **one another**. = They waited for each other.

4.9 Demonstrative pronouns

this	TEACHER: **This** is the last time that I'm going to warn you not to arrive late for the beginning of the class.
that	PUPIL: You don't have to say **that**. Really! I've got a good excuse. First my motorbike broke down and then on my way I nearly had an accident.
those	TEACHER: **Those** are very poor excuses, I must say. I suppose your legs broke down on the other days when you were late?

——— form ———

pronoun (subject) pronoun (object)

this
that } + verb (singular)

these
those } + verb (plural)

verb + this
that } (singular)

verb + these
those } (plural)

this is near – that is further away

DEMONSTRATIVE PRONOUNS have the same form as
DEMONSTRATIVE ADJECTIVES (4.10). They do not, however,
stand in front of a noun. They stand alone:

Show me **that**!
Give me **those**!
These are not what I ordered.

that (a single thing or person)
those (several things or people)

We use **that** and **those** to show that the thing(s) we are talking
about is (are) at a distance from us in either time or space:

That is my teacher standing **at the bus stop**.
Were **those** your parents I saw you with **yesterday**?

this (a single thing or person)
these (several things or people)

We use **this** and **these** to show that the thing(s) we are talking
about is (are) near to us in either time or space:

This is a much nicer colour than **that**.
I don't like **those**. I prefer **these** because they're leather.

4.10 Demonstrative adjectives

that	CUSTOMER: I'd like to buy a new car. **That** blue Renault looks quite interesting over there. How much is it?
that this	SALESMAN: **That** car is £2000 but I think we have a better one to offer you. **This** Datsun here is the same price but it's a lot newer. And there are lots of extras to go with it.
those	CUSTOMER: Well, what about **those** Italian cars in the forecourt?
these	SALESMAN: Well, sir, I think that **these** cars in the showroom are our best buys.

---
form

| this
that } + noun (singular) | these
those } + noun (plural) |

USE

near – further away

DEMONSTRATIVE ADJECTIVES have the same form as the corresponding PRONOUNS (4.9) and are used in a similar way to suggest nearness or distance. But they are followed by a noun and cannot stand alone:

This book (here, near to me) is very interesting, but **that book** (over there, further away from me) is very boring.

These houses (near to us) are new, but **those houses** (further away from us) are really very old.

That house we saw **yesterday** was too small, but **this** one (today) looks much bigger.

 It is not necessary to repeat the noun being described. Instead we can use **one**:

That house we saw yesterday was too small, but **this one** looks much bigger.

4.11 Bird's eye box: Reciprocal/demonstrative pronouns and demonstrative adjectives

We haven't spoken to **each other** for years.	⟶ reciprocal pronoun
This is the last time I'm going to accept it.	⟶ demonstrative pronoun
That car belongs to me.	⟶ demonstrative adjective

4.12 Relative pronouns

who

that

of which

BRIAN: Do you remember the teacher **who** had been working in the Soviet Union before he came to this school?

JOE: Do you mean the one **that** got the job in Indonesia?

BRIAN: Yes, I mean Alistair. Well, when he arrived in Indonesia to begin his new job he had a whole series of problems **of which** accommodation was apparently the greatest.

which

JOE: What happened to him?
BRIAN: When he arrived there he was given an address to
go to. It was a large house **which** was supposed to be
divided into three flats.
JOE: And somebody was already living there?
BRIAN: No. They hadn't even started to build the house!

--- **form** ---

relative pronoun

who
whom
which
Noun phrase + that + extra information
whose
of which
of whom

USE 1

Giving extra information about a noun

We use **who, whom, which, that, whose, of which, of whom**
to connect two pieces of information. The second piece usually
gives us extra information about the first. The first piece can be
a sentence or a NOUN PHRASE (2.1):

1
That is the swimmer.

2
She won the gold medal.

We can connect these two sentences by using a RELATIVE
PRONOUN:

That's the swimmer **who** won the gold medal.

1
I was talking to the men.

2
Their cars were stolen.

→ I was talking to the men **whose** cars were stolen.

1 A relative pronoun can replace a SUBJECT PRONOUN (4.1):

Jack is the man. **He** works for a big computer company.
⟶ Jack is the man **who** works for a big computer company.

A relative pronoun can also replace an OBJECT PRONOUN
(4.1.1):

This is the shirt. I bought **it** last week.
⟶ This is the shirt **which** I bought last week.

39

USE 2

who (subject)

We use **who** when we want to give extra information about people. **who** is usually the subject of the extra information:

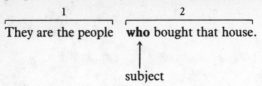

USE 3

who/whom (object)

who can also be the object of the extra information:

She is the girl. I met her yesterday afternoon.
She is the girl **who** I met yesterday afternoon.

In everyday speech we often put the preposition at the end of the information clause:

That is the teacher **who** I was talking **to**.

 2 A CLAUSE is a group of words containing a main verb. A MAIN CLAUSE makes complete sense and can stand alone:

He is coming (. . .).

A SUBORDINATE CLAUSE cannot stand alone. Its meaning is dependent on the main clause:

. . . after he has finished work.

 3 In formal and business English **whom** is always used as the personal object pronoun, and in this case the preposition always precedes the relative pronoun:

Is that the clerk **to whom** you gave the documents?

USE 4

which

We use **which** when we want to give extra information about things, animals or ideas. It can be the subject or object of the extra clause:

She is interested in any idea **which** can bring her money.
This is the grammar **which** I was telling you about.

USE 5

that

We use **that** when we want to give extra information about people, things, animals or ideas. It can be the subject or object of the extra clause:

Probably he's the man **that** (who) will become president.

It's one of the houses **that** (which) was bombed during the war.

Is he the boy **that** (who) you were arguing with?

Notice that we can use **that** in place of **who** and **which** (**which** is considered more formal than **that**).

 4 If **who, which** or **that** is the object of the information clause then it is very common to omit the relative pronoun:

Here is the book. I read it yesterday.

i Here is the book **that** I read yesterday. ⎫ Both sentences
ii Here is the book I read yesterday. ⎭ are acceptable.

In conversation, sentence **ii** is much more common.

USE 6

whose

      1   2

John is the fellow.   His daughter studies physics at Oxford.
John is the fellow **whose** daughter studies physics at Oxford.

whose shows that the **daughter** belongs to the **fellow**. We use **whose** to show that something or someone belongs to a person or people:

He is the man **whose** window you broke.
⟶ The window belongs to the man.

The women **whose** credit cards were stolen went to the police.
⟶ The credit cards belong to the women.

USE 7

of which

of which can be used to show possession by a thing or things, but in practice we avoid this construction if possible:

Every book **of which** the **cost** is more than £5 should be reduced.
⟶ Every book **costing** more than £5 should be reduced.

This is the town the main street **of which** was widened last year.
⟶ This is the town **where** the main street was widened last year.

4.13 Bird's eye box: Relative pronouns

who whom which that
whose of which of whom $\longrightarrow$ relative pronouns

We all know the man **whom**
we are talking about.

We all know the man we are $\longrightarrow$ no relative pronoun
talking about.   necessary

4.14   Emphatic pronouns (—self)

ourselves
yourself
myself

themselves

JOHN: We certainly need a kitchen cupboard for all the
plates and things.
MARY: Yes, but they're so expensive. Of course, we
could build it **ourselves**.
JOHN: You mean we should get a Do It **Yourself** kit?
MARY: Yes. I'd prefer to try to build one **myself**, but
perhaps you don't like the idea.
JOHN: No, I think we can do it if we follow the
instructions. After all, the people next door built a
complete garage **themselves** so it shouldn't be too
difficult to put a cupboard together.

— **form** —

pronoun (subject)   emphatic pronoun

I $\longrightarrow$ my		myself
you $\longrightarrow$ your		yourself
he $\longrightarrow$ him	+ **self** $\rightarrow$	himself	(singular)
she $\longrightarrow$ her		herself
it $\longrightarrow$ it		itself
one $\longrightarrow$ one		oneself

we $\longrightarrow$ our		ourselves
you $\longrightarrow$ your	+ **selves** $\rightarrow$	yourselves	(plural)
they $\longrightarrow$ them		themselves

USE

Emphasis

We use an EMPHATIC PRONOUN to give extra importance to
the NOUN (2.1) or PRONOUN (4.1) subject of a sentence:

I repaired the motor car **myself**.
The woman telephoned for the police **herself**.

In the examples the speaker wants to emphasize the fact that **I** repaired the car and **the woman** telephoned the police, and not somebody else.

 1 For an even stronger effect, the emphatic pronoun can come directly after the subject:

The teacher **himself** gave the petition to the Prime Minister.

 2 When we pronounce emphatic pronouns we put the stress on the word **self**:

I mys**elf** . . .
She hers**elf** . . .

4.15 Reflexive pronouns (—self)

herself

yourself

herself, yourselves

SHOPPER: Quick! There's been an accident. An old lady's just fallen down the escalator in the shop. She's hurt **herself**. I feel dreadful. I tried to stop her falling, but I couldn't.

STORE MANAGER: All right now. Don't blame **yourself**! Look she's begining to come round. She's talking to **herself**. Could you other people move **yourselves** out of the way. We don't want to shock the old lady.

─────────── **form** ───────────

subject +	verb +	reflexive pronoun +	(other information)
I	wash	myself	(every day).
You	behaved	yourself	(very badly).
He	saw	himself	(in the mirror).
We	pushed	ourselves	(too much).

subject +	verb +	(other information)	+ preposition +	reflexive pronoun
My sister	talks		to	herself.

He	bought	the present	for	himself.
We	are not	satisfied	with	ourselves.
You	can look		after	yourselves.
They	are talking		among(st)	themselves.

REFLEXIVE PRONOUNS have the same form as EMPHATIC PRONOUNS (4.14).

USE 1

Subject and object the same

We use —**self** after a VERB (see Chapters 9 and 11) when the subject and object of a sentence are the same person or thing:

Paul reminded himself not to argue with his father.

They enjoyed **themselves** on the beach.

USE 2

After prepositions

(See Chapter 21 for PREPOSITIONS.)

We can use —**self** after prepositions:

They must learn to look **after themselves**.
We kept the information **to ourselves**.

4.16 Bird's eye box: Emphatic/reflexive pronouns

myself yourself himself herself itself oneself ourselves yourselves themselves	⟶ emphatic/reflexive pronouns
I will solve the problem **myself**.	⟶ emphasis of subject
The President **himself** gave the news.	
You take **yourself** too seriously.	⟶ reflexive pronoun after a verb
She worries about **herself**.	⟶ reflexive pronoun after a preposition

4.17   Indefinite pronouns

somebody
something

nobody
nothing
everything

someone

> CAROLINE: Jake! I heard **somebody** downstairs. There's **something** happening in the living-room. It must be a thief.
>
> JAKE: There's **nobody** downstairs. You're just imagining it. Anyway, there's **nothing** in this house that's worth stealing. And we've insured **everything** that we've bought.
>
> CAROLINE: That isn't the point. I don't like the idea of **someone** wandering around our house in the middle of the night! Go and have a look!

— **form** —

somebody	anybody	nobody	everybody
somibody somebody			
somebody	anybody	nobody	everybody
someone	anyone	no one	everyone
something	anything	nothing	everything

USE 1

Talking about unspecified people or things – somebody/anybody, someone/anyone, something/anything

As a general guide we use these words according to whether the sentence is a positive statement, a question or a negative sentence:

positive ——→ There's **somebody** looking at your car.   **+**

negative ——→ There is**n't anybody** with him tonight.   **–**

question ——→ Is **anybody** going to buy it?   **?**

There's **somebody** looking at your car.
——→ There is a person (a person we don't know) looking at your car.

There is**n't anybody** with him tonight.
⟶ There isn't a person (there is **nobody**) with him tonight.

We can use **someone** in the same way as we use **somebody**.
Anyone is also an alternative for **anybody**.

Something in my shoe is hurting my foot.
⟶ There is a thing (I don't know what it is) in my shoe
hurting my foot.

DETECTIVE: **Somebody** must have been there. I can see
footprints.
POLICEMAN: I can't see **anybody** and I can't see **anything** like
a footprint.
DETECTIVE: Look! There's **something** over there in the
grass.

USE 2

nobody, no one, nothing

nobody = **no one**

Nobody has checked my car. ⎫ These mean
No one has checked my car. ⎭ the same.

⟶ No person has checked my car. (It hasn't been checked.)

Nothing has been paid yet.
⟶ Not a thing (not anything, no amount or quantity) has
been paid yet.

MR JONES: Were there any calls for me today?
MRS JONES: No. **Nobody** phoned at all. There was a call
yesterday, but the man said it was **nothing**
important so he rang off.

USE 3

everybody, everyone, everything

everybody = **everyone**

We use **everyone** or **everybody** when we want to refer to all
the people in a group.

Everybody on the train should have a ticket. ⎫ These mean
Everyone on the train should have a ticket. ⎭ the same.

⟶ Each person (every person, all the people) on the train
should have a ticket.

Notice that **everyone/everybody** (subject) is followed by a
singular verb:

Everyone in the class likes chocolate.
Everybody is ready to go home.

46

Everybody has a ticket.

everything

We use **everything** when we mean 'all (the) things'. As the subject of a sentence it is also followed by a singular verb:

Everything depends on whether we can save the money.
She can see **everything** much more clearly now.
Everything was ready for the party.

4.17.1 Indefinite pronouns + else

everybody else

anything else

anybody else

something else

CAREERS OFFICER: You'll be leaving school in six
 months. **Everybody else** in your class has arranged a job
 or knows what they want to do. What about you?
PUPIL: I want to be a pilot in the air force. I'm not
 interested in **anything else**.
CAREERS OFFICER: But what about the qualifications
 you'll need? Have you spoken to **anybody else** about
 this? A-levels are essential if you want to be a pilot
 these days. Isn't there **something else** you could apply
 for as well?

——— **form** ———

indefinite pronoun + else

somebody	else
anyone	else
nothing	else
everything	else
etc.	

USE 4

An extra/different one

else means 'in addition to, another, a different'. We often use it with this meaning after INDEFINITE PRONOUNS:

Somebody else took the money.
⟶ Another (a different) person took the money.

I didn't want this present. I wanted something else.
⟶ I didn't want this present. I wanted another (a different) one.

Can you think of anybody else?
⟶ Can you think of another (a different) person?

No one else will help me now.
⟶ No other person will help me now.

It's too late. There's nothing else we can do.
⟶ It's too late. There's no other thing (there isn't another thing) that we can do.

NOTE

somewhere, anywhere, nowhere and **everywhere** are ADVERBS OF PLACE (7.3), but they are used in the same way as indefinite pronouns.

There isn't anywhere to put my coat.
It's so noisy here. Can we go somewhere else?

See also QUESTION WORDS Chapter 5 + ELSE, 5.1.1.

4.18   Bird's eye box: Indefinite pronouns

somebody/someone (people) ⟶ unidentified, positive
something (things)   sentences

Somebody here could tell
you the answer.

anybody/anyone (people) ⟶ unidentified, negative
anything (things)   sentences and questions

He did**n't** see **anyone** all
day.

Is there **anything** I can do?

nobody/no one (people)   ⟶ 'no people/things',
nothing (things)   positive sentences

Nobody could help us.

everybody/everyone   ⟶ 'all (the) people/things',
(people)   positive and negative
everything (things)   sentences and questions

Everybody arrived on time.

I have**n't** seen **everyone**
yet.

Did you put **everything**
away?

It was **somebody else**, not ⟶ indefinite
me.   pronoun + **else**

5 QUESTION WORDS

CONTENTS

5.1 Question words

what . . . ?

what . . . ?

how . . . ?
where . . . ?
why . . . ?

ROY: Jenny, **what** are you doing today? Perhaps we could go to the swimming pool together.

JENNY: **What** time do you want to go?

ROY: Well, I'm meeting Bryan at ten o'clock.

JENNY: That's in fifteen minutes. **How** are you going to get there in time? And **where** are you meeting him?

ROY: At the swimming pool. Let's see. **Why** don't you drive us there? Then you'll have to come swimming too!

form

question word + verb (positive)

What	is happening?
Who	is shouting?

question word + verb (question form)

What	are you doing?
Who	do you mean?
Where	are the glasses?
When	is she coming?
Which	do you want?
Why	did you tell her?
Whose	is this pen?
How	are they travelling?

USE

Asking about people and things

When we want to ask a question about things, people, places, etc. we use QUESTION WORDS (INTERROGATIVES):

JOHN: **What**'s the time, David?
DAVID: It's half past eight.

We use question words in the following ways:

what? ⟶ questions about things or actions
'**What**'s that floating on the water?' 'It's a piece of wood.'

who? ⟶ questions about people
'**Who**'s coming to the meeting today?' 'Mr Smith is.'

where? ⟶ questions about place
'**Where**'s she going to study?' 'In Rome.'

when? ⟶ questions about time
'**When** shall we meet tonight?' 'At six o'clock.'

which? ⟶ questions about choice
'**Which** do you like, the blue one or the green one?' 'The green one.'

why? ⟶ questions about reasons
'**Why** should I pay for the meal?' 'Because you've eaten it!'

whose? ⟶ questions about possession
'**Whose** is this book?' 'It's mine.'

how? ⟶ questions about means or methods
'**How** can I get to Birmingham from here?' 'By train.'

⟶ questions about frequency, quantity, or distance
'**How** often do you go to the cinema?' 'Twice a week.'
'**How** much money have you got?' 'A thousand pounds.'
'**How** far is it to London?' 'Thirty miles.'

5.1.1 Question words with else

 We can add **else** to question words to give a sense of **'extra'**, **'also'** or **'in addition'**:

What else do you want to drink?
$\longrightarrow$ What other thing do you want to drink?

Who else is coming to the meeting?
$\longrightarrow$ Which other person is coming to the meeting?

| DANGER | We do not use **else** with **whose**.

5.2 Interrogative adjectives

which one . . .
which brochure . . .

what sort . . .

what price . . .

> JENNY: There are lots of interesting package holidays in this brochure. **Which one** shall we book?
> JOHN: First of all **which brochure** are you looking at? That's last year's.
> JENNY: Oh. Here's the new one. **What sort** of holiday would you like?
> JOHN: I'd really like to lie in the sun, have the occasional swim and then spend the evenings in wonderful restaurants.
> JENNY: And **what price** have you got in mind?
> JOHN: That's the only problem! As little as possible!

─────── **form** ───────

interrogative adjective	+ noun	+ verb (question form)
What	sort	do you want?
Which	car	shall we buy?
Whose	pen	is this?

| USE | **Identifying a person or thing**

We use **what** in front of a singular or plural NOUN (2.1–2.3.4) when we want some information about it:

MR SMITH: **What** answer did you give when the policeman asked you for your address?
MR JONES: Well, I told him the truth, that I haven't a permanent address at the moment.

ALICE: **What** monuments did you visit?
ROY: I only had time to visit Stonehenge.

We use **which** in front of a singular or plural noun when we are asking about one thing out of a number of things. **Which** is more restrictive than **what**:

Which (of these) cities have you visited?
(The speaker is thinking of several particular cities.)

What cities have you visited?
(The speaker is not thinking of any particular cities at all.)

Sometimes the difference between **which?** and **what?** is very slight, but if you use **of these** or **of them** you must use **which?**:

These holidays all look interesting. **Which** of them shall we choose?

We use **whose** in front of a singular or plural noun when we want to find out who owns something:

KEN: **Whose** purse is this?
LINDA: Oh, it's mine! It must've fallen out of my handbag.

5.3 Exclamations

 what and **how** can be used to make exclamations:

What bad weather!
What a bad situation!
How terrible!
How expensive!

5.4 Bird's eye box: Question words

what? who? where?
when? which? why?   ⟶   question words
whose? how?

What are you discussing?
Who pays the bills?

What else did she say?   ⟶   question word + **else**
Which hotel do you like   ⟶   interrogative adjective
best?

6 ADJECTIVES

CONTENTS   *page*

6.1   Adjectives in front of nouns

best way, good
curry, lean meat
hot curry
dry curry
white rice
brown rice, cold
water, spicy curry

> The **best way** to make a **good curry** is to buy some **lean meat** and cook it slowly with the curry spices and some liquid. If you like **hot curry** you can add chilli – but be careful! You should add plenty of liquid because a **dry curry** can be difficult to eat. **White rice** is usually better than **brown rice** with a curry. A glass of **cold water** is all you will need to drink with a **spicy curry**!

—————————— **form** ——————————

(article/quantifier) + adjective + noun (singular/plural)

the	black	dog
a	big	house
some	foreign	students
—	cheap	petrol
—	fast	cars

USE

Describing (giving extra information about) things or people

When we want to give some extra information about things or people (see Chapter 2 for NOUNS) we can do this with the help of one or more ADJECTIVES. We put adjectives in front of nouns:

adjective   noun

They bought a **beautiful** house.

adjective   noun

She's drinking a **strong** cup of tea.

adjective noun

He crashed because he had an   **old**   car.

 In English, an adjective does not need to agree with its noun, so it does not change when it is used with a plural noun:

A **red** car. ⟶ Ten **red** cars.
A **happy** child. ⟶ Fifteen **happy** children.

6.2 Adjectives after *be*

was tall is difficult
is dark

was tall/thin
was black, am sure

POLICEMAN: Can you describe the man you saw running away yesterday evening?
WOMAN: Yes, I think he **was tall**. But it's **difficult** to be sure. Our street's very **dark**.
POLICEMAN: Try to remember something about him.
WOMAN: He **was tall** and very **thin**. And I think his hair **was black**, but I'm not **sure**.

--- **form** ---

(pro)noun (subject) + **be** + adjective

It	is	early.
We	are	tired.
The weather	was	cold.
The guests	were	late.

USE

We can use an adjective to give extra information about a noun when we put the adjective after the verb **be** (9.2–9.3):

JIM: What colour is the sky outside?
PETER: It's very **grey**.

 We also use adjectives predicatively – that is, after these verbs:

become (when it means 'begin to be') feel look
smell taste sound seem appear stay

(pro)noun	+ verb	+ adjective
That perfume	smells	lovely.
I	feel	sick.
The situation	is becoming	difficult.

You're **looking unhappy**. What's wrong?

Your pizza **tastes** really **good**.

Stay quiet and nobody will hear you.

6.3 Adjectives as nouns

USE 1

Some adjectives can be used to describe groups of people (3.3):

The young and **the energetic** swam in the sea.

USE 2

Some nationality adjectives can be used as nouns:

The Swiss are famous for their chocolate.
The English are famous for their rain!

Apart from **the Swiss**, these are restricted to those adjectives which end in —**ch** (**the French**), —**ese** (**the Chinese**) and some which end in —**ish** (**the Spanish**).

USE 3

The SUPERLATIVE form of some ADJECTIVES (6.6) can be used as an ABSTRACT NOUN (2.1):

This is **the best** I can do. (the best work/effort)
Have you heard **the latest**? (the latest news)
He's always expecting **the worst**. (the worst event/consequence)

6.4 Bird's eye box: Adjectives

She is a **sensitive person**.	$\longrightarrow$	adjective in front of a noun
This person **is sensitive**.	$\longrightarrow$	adjective after **be**
They **look** very **good**.	$\longrightarrow$	adjective after **look, get, smell, taste**, etc.
That's **the worst** you could do.	$\longrightarrow$	adjective as a noun

6.5 Comparative adjectives

heavier

cheaper

more expensive

wider
fresher
quicker

VAL: Hello, Pam. This bag's getting **heavier** and **heavier**! I've just been to the supermarket and it's a long walk, but the food's **cheaper** than at the local shops.

PAM: I don't agree with you, actually. The cheese and some of the biscuits are **more expensive** than in our corner shop.

VAL: You may be right. But you get a **wider** range in the big shops and the food's **fresher** because they have a **quicker** turnover.

form

adjective + **er/r** + noun			**more** + adjective + noun		
small	er	houses	more	beautiful	girls
tall	er	men	more	interesting	books
large	r	cities	more	important	items

1 When an adjective is short (one syllable) we usually make the COMPARATIVE form by putting **er/r** on the end:

short ⟶ short**er**   long ⟶ long**er**

When an adjective is long (three syllables or more) we usually put **more** before it:

interesting ⟶ **more** interesting
intelligent ⟶ **more** intelligent

Adjectives of two syllables follow one or other of the above rules. As a guide, two-syllable adjectives ending in **ful**, **ing** or **re** usually take **more**:

care**ful** ⟶ **more** careful   unsure ⟶ **more** unsure

Two-syllable adjectives ending in **er**, **ow**, **le** or **y** (see also ☞ 3) usually add **er** in the comparative:

clever ⟶ clever**er**   shallow ⟶ shall**ower**

pretty ⟶ prettier
attractive ⟶ more attractive

57

2 Adjectives ending with a single vowel before a consonant double the consonant before adding **er**:

big ⟶ bi**gg**er

fat ⟶ fa**tt**er

Your jacket is much **bigger** than mine.

Tom is much **fatter** than Tim.

3 When an adjective ends in consonant + **y** we make the comparative form by adding **er** and also changing the **y** to **i**:

happy ⟶ happ**ier**   pretty ⟶ prett**ier**

USE

Comparing two things/people

We use the comparative form of an adjective followed by **than** (23.7) when we want to compare two things or people:

1   comparison   2

This table was **more expensive than** the chair.

1   comparison   2

My writing is **clearer than** yours.

my house

your house

My house is larger than yours (is).

See 23.7 for further COMPARISON LINKING WORDS.

6.5.1 Irregular comparatives

 The following adjectives have special comparative forms:

good	⟶	better
bad	⟶	worse
far	⟶	farther/further
many much	⟶	more

I couldn't imagine a **worse** situation than this.

She's a **better** organizer than I am.

I always drink **more** coffee and eat **more** biscuits just before examinations! It must be nerves.

6.6 Superlative adjectives

the most
impressive
the best equipped
the most modern
the loveliest
the most beautiful

When I was living in the Soviet Union **the most impressive** things I saw were the sports halls. They were **the best equipped** that I had ever used. **The most modern** sports halls were in the universities. **The loveliest** city I stayed in was Kiev. It had **the most beautiful** avenues of trees I have ever walked along.

——————— **form** ———————

the + adjective	+ **est**	+ noun
the	green_____	_est	tree
the	long_____	_est	rivers
the	full_____	_est	glass

the + **most**	+ adjective	+ noun
the	most	interesting	things
the	most	dangerous	person
the	most	compact	dictionary

 The rules for forming the SUPERLATIVE of adjectives are related to those for the COMPARATIVE (6.5):

Adjectives which take **er/r** in the comparative take **est** in the superlative.
Adjectives which take **more** in the comparative take **most** in the superlative.

Contrast

SHORT ADJECTIVES		LONGER ADJECTIVES	
warm	⟶ the warm**est**	difficult	⟶ the **most** difficult
old	⟶ the old**est**	hurtful	⟶ the **most** hurtful
tall	⟶ the tall**est**	boring	⟶ the **most** boring

The longest day of the year is in June.

The most interesting way to travel nowadays is by train.

Leaving her was **the most hurtful** thing he could do.

The happiest time of my life was my childhood.*

The biggest mistake I ever made was to marry at eighteen.*

*See 6.5 (☞ 1–3) for spelling rules.

Two-syllable adjectives which take **er** and **est** can also be used with **more** and **most**:

polite   stupid   pleasant   common   clever

The most common mistake we make is not to listen to others.
or
The commonest mistake we make is not to listen to others.

NOTE

A superlative adjective can be preceded by:
the definite article (3.2) ⟶ **the** longest day
a possessive adjective (4.5) ⟶ **my** best attempt
the + a possessive noun (2.4) ⟶ **the school's** largest building

USE

Comparing three or more things/people

We use the superlative form of an adjective when we compare more than two things or people:

    1   2   3

I visited Moscow, Kiev and Leningrad. **The most enjoyable** time was when I was in Kiev.

6.6.1 Irregular superlatives

Those adjectives which have a special comparative form (6.5.1) also have a special superlative form:

```
good      ⟶   (the) best
bad       ⟶   (the) worst
far       ⟶   (the) farthest (the) furthest
many ⎫
much ⎭    ⟶   (the) most
```

The farthest point from Scotland in Britain is Land's End in the south-west.

My best school report arrived the day that I left.

The most expensive cake does not have to be **the best** (cake).

6.7 Bird's eye box: Comparative/superlative adjectives

He has a chea**per** car.	⟶ comparative, short adjective
She has a **more** beautiful car.	⟶ comparative, long adjective
We had **the** great**est** luck.	⟶ superlative, short adjective
It was **the most** important day.	⟶ superlative, long adjective

7 ADVERBS

CONTENTS

7.1 Adverbs of definite time

today

> GEORGE: The police visited my house **today**. They were
> looking for stolen jewels.
> PETER: Stolen jewels? Why on earth did they choose
> your house?
> GEORGE: Apparently somebody phoned the police
> **yesterday** and told them I had something to do with it.
> PETER: Did they find anything?
> GEORGE: Of course not, but they said they were coming
> back again **tomorrow**.

yesterday

tomorrow

─── form ───

ADVERBS	ADVERBIAL PHRASES
today	two days ago
tomorrow	last week
yesterday	next week
	etc.

USE

Information about when

An ADVERB (or ADVERBIAL PHRASE) OF DEFINITE TIME
answers the question **when?**. The time it tells us about is fairly
precise:

The letter arrived **yesterday**.
When did the letter arrive? ⟶ **Yesterday**.

Yesterday is a definite time adverb. In this example it tells us
when the letter arrived.

The results of the exam will arrive **at the end of the week**.
When will the results arrive? ⟶ **At the end of the week**.

At the end of the week is a definite time adverbial phrase. It
tells us **when** the results will arrive.

7.1.1 Position of definite time adverbs

Adverbs or adverbial phrases of definite time can stand at the
beginning of a sentence or clause or at the end:

Yesterday I crossed the English Channel on the ferry.
They visited the British Museum **last week**.

The end position is more common.

7.2 Adverbs of indefinite time and frequency/duration

nowadays
sometimes
occasionally

never

before

TIM: Do you do anything to keep fit **nowadays**?
DAVID: Yes, I still go jogging every morning. **Sometimes** I even go twice a day and **occasionally** even three times!
TIM: But you **never** seem to get any thinner.
DAVID: What do you mean? I weighed eighty kilos **before** and now I only weigh seventy-five.

form

TIME	FREQUENCY/DURATION
already*	ever
afterwards	never
before	continually
beforehand	frequently
early	rarely
just*	often
late	occasionally
nowadays	sometimes
soon	always
still	
yet	

*See also 11.17.1 (☞) for use with the PRESENT PERFECT TENSE.

USE

Information about when/how often/how long

Adverbs of indefinite time

An ADVERB OF INDEFINITE TIME answers the question **when?**. The time it tells us about is not very precise:

You must take a test **before** you can have a driving licence.
When must you take a test? ⟶ **Before** you can have a licence.

He always arrives **late** for class.
When does he arrive for class? ⟶ **Late**.

Adverbs of frequency/duration

An ADVERB OF FREQUENCY/DURATION answers the question **how often?/how long?**:

I **never** eat meat – I'm a vegetarian.
How often do I eat meat? ⟶ **Never**.

He's **always** lived in Paris.
How long has he lived in Paris? ⟶ **Always**.

7.2.1 Position of indefinite time and frequency/duration adverbs

We often find the following adverbs in the middle of a sentence or clause:

> already just still often always never ever soon
> frequently not yet

They appear typically between the AUXLIARY VERB (9.2.3) and the main verb (before the main verb when there is no auxiliary):

subject	auxiliary	adverb	main verb
She	has	already	left.
They	have	just	paid.
I	am	still	living here.
We	will	never	learn.
We	will	soon	finish.
I	haven't	yet*	heard (yet).
We	have	always	known.
auxiliary	*subject*		
Have	you	ever*	worked?

*ever and yet usually appear in the negative form of questions, with yet at the end of a clause, and ever between the subject and main verb.
Haven't you read that book yet?
Won't you ever see her?

 In spoken English the auxiliary is usually abbreviated:

They **have** just arrived. ⟶ They've just arrived.
He **will** soon learn. ⟶ He'll soon learn.

7.3 Adverbs of place

down below,
inside
here
throughout, near

outside

JACK: Something's wrong with the car again. There's oil leaking out **down below** and when I looked **inside** there was a strange smell.
GARAGE MECHANIC: Well. Leave it **here** and I'll check the engine **throughout**. As you work so **near**, you can collect it at the end of the day.
JACK: Thanks a lot. I'll see you **outside** at 5.30.

---

form

ADVERBS		ADVERBIAL PHRASES
above	here	down below
backwards	inside	in front of
behind	near	over there
below	nowhere	up above
close	out	
everywhere	outside	
far	there	
forwards	throughout	

USE

Information about where

An ADVERB (or adverbial phrase) OF PLACE answers the question **where?**.

MOTHER: **Where** are you, Kathryn?

KATHRYN: I'm **inside**. It's too hot **outside** so I decided to find some shade **here**.

ROBERT: **Where** did you put my glasses, Janet? I can't find them **anywhere**.

JANET: Your glasses are **over there**, just **in front of** you.

7.3.1 Position of adverbs of place

Adverbs or adverbial phrases of place usually stand at the end of a sentence or clause:

I can't see anybody **down below**.
How long have you been living **there**?

If there is also a time adverb, this goes at the end or beginning of the sentence or clause:

       place   time

I couldn't see anybody **down there yesterday**.

or time   place

Yesterday I couldn't see anybody **down there**.

66

7.4 Adverbs of manner

badly

particularly well
quickly,
professionally

> JOHN: Our football team is playing very **badly** today.
> They haven't played a good game of football all
> season.
> ROY: Now, be fair. The visiting team is playing
> **particularly well.** You can't expect success to come
> **quickly.** The team's only been playing **professionally**
> for six months.
> JOHN: That's no excuse for terrible football!

---
form
---

adjective + **ly** | adjective −**y**   + **ily**

stupid___ly | easy ——→eas___ily
strange___ly | lazy ——→laz___ily
bad___ly | happy ——→happ___ily

- -

adjective −**e** + **ly** | adjective + **ally**

true ——→tru___ly | scientific___ally
due ——→du___ly | economic___ally
whole ——→whol__ly | angelic___ally

USE 1

Information about how

An ADVERB OF MANNER answers the question **how?** or **in
what way?**:

The sprinter ran very **quickly.**
How did the sprinter run? ——→ **Quickly.**

The bell rang **loudly.**
How did the bell ring? ——→ **Loudly.**

He rows **smoothly.** They played **efficiently.** You typed **quickly.**

USE 2

Information about how (much)/to what extent

Some adverbs, such as **very, extremely, really, quite, fairly,**
tell us something about an adjective or another adverb rather
than about a verb. They answer the question **how (much)?/to
what extent?**:

She is **extremely** intelligent.
How intelligent is she? ——→ **Extremely.**

He drove **very** slowly.
How slowly did he drive? ——→ **Very.**

7.4.1 Irregular adverbs of manner

adjective		adverb
good	⟶	well
fast	⟶	fast
hard	⟶	hard

7.5 Restriction adverbs (emphasizing with word order)

only

under no circumstances
never

RONALD: Dad, I think we should go out for a meal today.

FATHER: Well, **only** once or twice a year do I eat out in restaurants, and it's about five months since I last ate out – so, why not? Where shall we go then?

RONALD: There are some good Indian restaurants in the centre of town.

FATHER: Ron, **under no circumstances** am I going to eat that sort of food. **Never** will I eat in a foreign restaurant. You should know me better than that! Give me good, plain English cooking every time!

─── **form** ───

ADVERBS	ADVERBIAL PHRASES
hardly	in no way
never	in vain
only	no sooner . . . than
rarely	so + adjective or adverb
scarcely	under no circumstances
seldom	

USE

Emphasizing certain adverbs

When we put the adverbs **never, rarely, seldom**, etc. *at the beginning* of a sentence, we give them more importance. We must also change the order of the other words – we put the MODAL VERB (see Chapter 10) or AUXILIARY VERB (9.2.3–4) in second place:

adverbial
phrase auxiliary subj.

In no way would I **ever** steal anything.

adverbial phrase   auxiliary subj.

Hardly   had   he come through the door when the bomb exploded.

adverbial phrase   auxiliary subj.

Only then   did   she realize it.

This is a very emphatic and rather formal way of speaking. By talking like this, the father in the dialogue sounds very pompous.

7.6 Adverbial phrase instead of adverb

We use an adverbial phrase with the words **way** or **manner** when it is difficult to form an adverb.

friendly ⟶ friendlily

He introduced himself to me **in a friendly way**.
She shouted at me **in an insulting manner**.

7.7 Adjective and adverb the same

Some words can be both an adjective and adverb:

daily	far	late	near
deep	fast	little	monthly
early	hard	long	weekly
enough	high	low	yearly

He's an **early** riser. (adjective)
I got up **early** this morning. (adverb)
It's a **fast** car. (adjective)
He drove the car **fast**. (adverb)

Notice that an adjective can sometimes end in **ly**.

7.8 Bird's eye box: Adverbs

He phoned **yesterday**.	⟶ adverb of definite time
I'll ring back **soon**.	⟶ adverb of indefinite time
He's **often** visited me.	⟶ adverb of frequency
I've **always** liked John.	⟶ adverb of duration
Go **downstairs** and phone.	⟶ adverb of place
He writes **untidily**.	⟶ adverb of manner

7.9 Comparative adverbs

harder

more successfully

more seriously

> STUDENT: I'm working **harder** than I did last year for my exams.
> TERRY: Well, I hope you'll pass them **more successfully** than you did last year!
> STUDENT: I ought to. I take my work much **more seriously** than I used to, so I hope I'll be all right.

---

form

adverb + **er**	**more** + adverb
deep_____er	more energetically
fast_____er	more intensively
hard_____er	more often

 With one-syllable adverbs we form the COMPARATIVE by adding **er**:

high ⟶ high**er**
low ⟶ low**er**

With **early** we form the comparative by adding **er** and also changing the **y** to **i**:

early ⟶ earl**ier**

With adverbs of two syllables or more the comparison is usually formed with **more**:

energetically ⟶ **more** energetically
intensively ⟶ **more** intensively

USE

Comparing two actions

We use the comparative form of an adverb followed by **than** when we want to compare two actions:

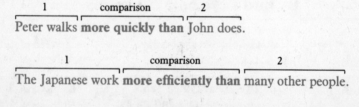

Peter walks **more quickly than** John does.

The Japanese work **more efficiently than** many other people.

Normally I go to bed **earlier than** my sister does.

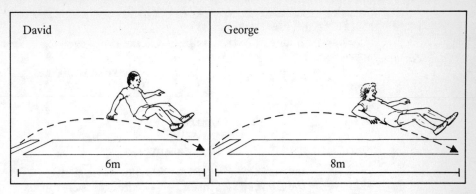

David

George

6m

8m

George jumped further than David.

See 23.7 for further COMPARISON LINKING WORDS.

7.9.1 Irregular comparatives

The following adverbs have special comparative forms:

well ⟶	better	a lot ⟶	more
badly ⟶	worse	little ⟶	less
much ⟶	more	far ⟶	farther/further

He did **worse** than he thought in the job interview.
I smoke **more** than I used to.

7.10 Superlative adverbs

most cheaply

PASSENGER: Could you tell me how I could travel **most cheaply** from London to Derby, please?
BOOKING CLERK: You could catch the 5.20 train. It gets you there **the quickest**. It also costs **the least**.
PASSENGER: It must be my lucky day!

the quickest, the
least

———— **form** ————

(the)	+ adverb	+ est		the	+ most	+ adverb
(the)	quick	est		the	most	stupidly
(the)	fast	est		the	most	cheaply
(the)	low	est		the	most	painfully

The rules for forming the SUPERLATIVE of adverbs are related to those for the COMPARATIVE (7.9).

Adverbs which take **er** in the comparative take **est** in the superlative.

Adverbs which take **more** in the comparative take **most** in the superlative.

Contrast

SHORT ADVERBS	LONGER ADVERBS
hard ⟶ the hard**est**	angrily ⟶ the **most** angrily
slow ⟶ the slow**est**	sensibly ⟶ the **most** sensibly
early ⟶ the earl**iest**	happily ⟶ the **most** happily

We have three very hardworking clerks, but Joanna works **the hardest**.

Bob Freeman talks **the most sensibly** of all the local politicians.

most before an adverb or adjective can also mean **very**:

He read the contract **most** carefully.
⟶ He read it **very** carefully.

It was a **most** interesting meeting.
⟶ It was **very** interesting.

USE

Comparing three or more actions

We use the superlative form of an adverb when we compare more than two actions with each other in order to show that one of them is faster, better, slower, etc. than all the others:

We have three motor cars but Peter's goes **the fastest**.
⟶ Peter's car is faster than all the others.

Paul earns a lot of money but John earns **the most** in the office.
⟶ John earns more than any other person in the office.

7.10.1 Irregular superlatives

Those adverbs which have a special comparative form (7.9.1) also have a special superlative form:

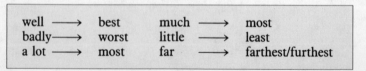

well ⟶	best	much ⟶	most
badly⟶	worst	little ⟶	least
a lot ⟶	most	far ⟶	farthest/furthest

He works **best** late at night.
In that class, it is Gordon who considers things (**the**) **most**
carefully.

  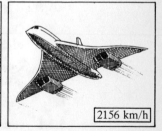

A car travels **fast**.

A train can go **faster** than a car.

Concorde travels **the fastest** (of all): twice the speed of sound.

Jan smiles **happily**.

Mary smiles **more happily** than Jan.

Jill smiles **the most happily** (of all).

7.11 Bird's eye box: Comparative/superlative adverbs of manner

She works har**der** than I do.	→ comparative, short adverb
She draws **more** beautifully than I do.	→ comparative, long adverb
Your child always shouts **the** loud**est**.	→ superlative, short adverb
This book is **the most** widely read in Japan.	→ superlative, long adverb

8 QUANTIFIERS

8.1 Quantifiers (large quantities)

In a dress shop

much

DAUGHTER: How **much** money have you got with you? I
want to buy that dress but I haven't got my cheque
book with me.

a lot of
many

MOTHER: Let me see. I seem to have **a lot of** coins in my
purse but not **many** notes. Ah yes! You're in luck – a
£20 note.

plenty of

DAUGHTER: Thanks, Mum. I'll give it back to you on
Thursday when I get paid. I'll have **plenty of** money
then.

--- **form** ---

quantifier	+ noun
much	time/money
many	people
a lot of	time/people
lots of	time/people
a great deal of	time/money
a number of	people
plenty of	time/people

USE

Large quantities

We use **much, many, a lot of, lots of**, etc. when we want to
say that there is a large number of things or a large amount of
something:

There are **many ways** of doing this.

We've already bought **lots of** Christmas **presents**.

MR SMITH: How **much time** have we got before the plane leaves?

MRS SMITH: We've got **lots of time**.
or We've got **plenty of time**.

When we want to use these QUANTIFIERS we must notice if the noun they refer to is COUNTABLE or UNCOUNTABLE:

Contrast	
COUNTABLE (NUMBER)	UNCOUNTABLE (AMOUNT)
We can see and count individual items:	We cannot see and count individual items:
many friends/chairs/apples	**much** time/petrol/sugar
Hence we ask the question:	Hence we ask the question:
How many friends have you got?	**How much** time have you got?
How many chairs/apples do you want?	**How much** petrol/sugar do you want?

We use **a lot of, lots of** and **plenty of** with both countable and uncountable nouns:

countable   uncountable

a lot of apples   a lot of water

Full information on the use of all these quantifiers is contained in the table on page 76.

> **Key:** − = negative sentence   + = positive sentence
> ? = question   c = countable nouns
> u/c = uncountable nouns

QUANTIFIER	EXAMPLES	NORMAL USE
much ⟶	I haven't **much** time. ⟶	− ⎫ u/c
⟶	Does she do **much** work? ⟶	? ⎭
many ⟶	I haven't **many** friends. ⟶	− ⎫
⟶	I have many friends. ⟶	+ ⎬ c
⟶	Does she have **many** friends? ⟶	? ⎭
a lot of ⟶	I haven't **a lot of** time. ⟶	− ⎫
⟶	I have **a lot of** friends. ⟶	+ ⎪
⟶	I have **a lot of** time. ⟶	+ ⎬ c u/c
⟶	Does she have **a lot of** friends? ⟶	? ⎭
lots of ⟶	I have **lots of** friends. ⟶	+ ⎫
⟶	I have **lots of** time. ⟶	+ ⎪
⟶	She doesn't have **lots of** money. ⟶	− ⎬ c u/c
⟶	Does she have **lots of** time? ⟶	? ⎭
a great deal of ⟶	They haven't **a great deal of** money. ⟶	− ⎫
⟶	I had **a great deal of** trouble parking the car. ⟶	+ ⎬ u/c
⟶	Does he really have **a great deal of** money? ⟶	? ⎭
a number of ⟶	I have **a number of** friends who live abroad. ⟶	+ c
plenty of ⟶	I have **plenty of** ideas. ⟶	+ ⎫ c u/c
⟶	Do you have **plenty of** time? ⟶	? ⎭

8.2 Quantifiers (small quantities)

RUTH: Whereabouts are we exactly? How far is it to Long Eaton?

a few

FRANK: Not far. We've only got **a few** miles left to do.

RUTH: Well, how many exactly? Look! There's very

little

little petrol left in the tank according to your petrol gauge.

FRANK: Oh dear! I don't think it'll be enough. We've

several

still got **several** miles to go before we get to the next petrol station. Let's stop the car and walk with the spare can.

RUTH: You can walk. I'll stay here and wait for you to come back.

—————— **form** ——————

quantifier + noun

a few/few	apples
a little/little	butter
several	apples

USE

Small quantities

We use a **a few, few, a little, little** and **several** when we want to say that there is only a small number of things or a small amount of something:

We have **a few** trees in our garden but not many.

She only takes **a little** sugar in her tea. She doesn't like a lot.

Again, we must notice whether the noun that a quantifier refers to is countable or uncountable. Full details are contained in the table on page 78.

> **Key:** − = negative sentence + = positive sentence
> ? = question c = countable nouns
> u/c = uncountable nouns

QUANTIFIER	EXAMPLES	NORMAL USE
a few ⟶ Meaning: not many, but some.	David has **a few** ideas ⟶ for a holiday but not many. Can I speak to you for **a few** minutes?	+ ⟶ ? } c
few ⟶ Meaning: a small number.	**Few** European people ⟶ can understand Chinese.	+ c
a little ⟶ Meaning: a small quantity. ⟶	I have **a little** cash left ⟶ but not a lot. D'you think I could use ⟶ **a little** of your petrol?	+ ? } u/c
little ⟶ Meaning: a small quantity.	Jane pays **little** attention⟶ to what she says.	+ u/c
several ⟶ Meaning: more than a few, but not many.	I met **several** very ⟶ interesting people on the train.	+ c

8.3 Quantifiers (neutral)

some KATHRYN: I want to go to town and buy **some** Christmas presents before it gets too crowded.
any JACKIE: It's a bit late. Haven't you bought **any** yet? I got most of mine last weekend. Where do you want to go?
some KATHRYN: Well, I'd really like to buy **some** cassettes
any for my brother. He hasn't got **any** good ones.
some JACKIE: OK. I'll come with you. Would you like **some** coffee before we go? It's pretty cold outside.

---
form

quantifier + noun

| some | drinks/water |
| any | drinks/water |

Neutral quantities

some
We use **some** in positive (+) sentences.

> **USE 1**

Before uncountable (u/c) nouns **some** means 'an amount of':

We have **some wood** in the cellar.
——→ We do not know exactly how **much** wood there is.

They have **some money** in the bank.

Jane bought **some wool** because she wanted to knit a pullover.

> **USE 2**

Before countable (c) nouns **some** means 'a number of':

The factory employs **some** skilled **workers**.
——→ We do not know exactly how **many** skilled workers there are.

I left **some books** on the table. Where are they now?

> **USE**

any
We use **any** in negative (−) sentences and in questions (?):

We don't have **any wood** in the cellar.
——→ There's no wood in the cellar.

They don't have **any money** in the bank.

Jane didn't buy **any wool** because she decided not to knit a pullover.

The factory doesn't employ **any** skilled **workers**.
——→ There are no skilled workers at the factory.

I didn't leave **any** books on the table.

Do you have **any wood** in the cellar?

Does the factory employ **any** skilled **workers**?

> **Key:** − = negative sentence   + = positive sentence
> ? = question   c = countable nouns
> u/c = uncountable nouns

Contrast

some			any		
We've got **some**	+	u/c	We haven't got **any**	−	u/c
wine.			wine.		
			Have we got **any** wine?	?	u/c
David has got **some** toys.	+	c	David hasn't got **any** toys.	−	c
			Has David got **any** toys?	?	c

8.3.1 *some* in question offers

 We use **some** in questions when we want to offer something to somebody – something which is part of a larger quantity:

MRS JONES: That coffee looks good. It's really strong.
MRS SMITH: There's plenty left. Would you like **some**?

8.4 Bird's eye box: Quantifiers

much (−   ?   u/c)
many (−   +   ?   c)
a lot of (−   +   ?   c   u/c)
lots of (−   +   ?   c   u/c)   } ⟶ large quantities
a great deal of (−   +   ?   u/c)
a number of (+   c)
plenty of (+   ?   c   u/c)

a few (+   ?   c)
few (+   c)
a little (+   ?   u/c)   } ⟶ small quantities
little (+   u/c)
several (+   c)

some (+   u/c   c)
any (−   ?   u/c   c)   } ⟶ neutral quantities

9 VERBS: BE, DO, HAVE

CONTENTS

9.1 Verbs (basic information)

> VERBS are words which tell us about ACTIONS and
> MOVEMENT: fly   write   run
> or about STATES: seem   be   become

In a dictionary we find the name of the verb – the INFINITIVE:

> speak   laugh   drink   become   sit   watch

81

Sometimes we put another verb in front of the infinitive to change its meaning. This extra verb is called a MODAL VERB (see Chapter 10):

I **can** speak.
He **must** come.

Or we add one or more letters to the infinitive:

He speak**s** every day.
She open**ed** the door quietly.

Or we change the verb:

speak ⟶ He **spoke** yesterday.
go ⟶ They **went** on holiday.
eat ⟶ We **ate** breakfast late.

Apart from 9.2–9.7, see Chapter 10 for MODAL VERBS and Chapter 11 for TENSES OF THE VERB.

9.2 be

was is are	There **was** a time when I wanted to travel all over the world. But it **is** difficult to do this. You must think about money and work. Some countries **are** also difficult to enter because you need a visa.
was were am	Fortunately, when I **was** a student I studied languages so there **were** lots of opportunities to work and travel at the same time. I **am** a teacher now but I **am** tired of moving around. At the moment I teach in Italy and I think I would like to stay here for ever.

─── **form** ───

PRESENT SIMPLE TENSE (11.3)

POSITIVE FORM · · · · We also have a SHORT FORM which we use very often when we speak:

I am	(a doctor).	I'm	(a doctor).	
You are	(a teacher).	you're	(a teacher).	
He ⎤		He's		(singular)
She ⎬ is	(tired).	She's	(tired).	
It ⎦		It's		
We ⎤	(late).	We're	(late).	
You ⎬ are	(teachers).	You're	(teachers).	(plural)
They ⎦	(students).	They're	(students).	

82

NEGATIVE FORM with **not** ──→ SHORT FORM		
I am not (a doctor).	I'm not . . .	
You are not (a teacher).	You're not . . .	
He |	He's |	(singular)
She | is not (tired).	She's | not . . .	
It |	It's |	
We | | (late).	We're |	
You | are not | (teachers).	You're |not . . .	(plural)
They| | (students).	They're|	

QUESTION FORM

(singular)	(plural)
Am I (early)?	Are we (late)?
Are you (a teacher)?	Are you (teachers)?
|he |	
Is | she | (tired)?	Are they (students)?
|it |	

9.2.1 *be* as a main verb (present simple tense)

USE 1

I am means 'I exist', 'This is my state'.

After **be** as a main verb we can put an ADJECTIVE (see Chapter 6):

(pro)noun (subject) + **be** + adjective		
He	is	tired.
She	is	happy.
Peter and Jane	are	tall.

or we can put a NOUN (see Chapter 2):

subject + **be** + noun		
He	is	an engineer.
They	are	policemen.
We	are	businessmen.

or we can put a PREPOSITION (see Chaper 21) plus noun:

subject	+ **be**	+ prep.	+ noun
You	are	at	work.
We	are	in	the classroom.
He	is	in	an office.

9.2.2 *be* as a main verb (past simple tense)

POSITIVE FORM

Yesterday I was (at home).
Last week you were (here).
    | he |
In 1980 | she | was (in Africa).   (singular)
    | it |

Yesterday we were (at home).
Last week you were (here).   (plural)
In 1980 they were (in Africa).

There is no short form of **be** in the past simple (positive).

NEGATIVE FORM (with **not**) ⟶ SHORT FORM

Yesterday I was not (at home).   I wasn't . . .
Last week you were not (here).   You weren't . . .
    | he | He |
In 1980 | she | was not (in Africa).   She | wasn't . . . (singular)
    | it | It |

Yesterday we were not (at home).   We weren't . . .
Last week you were not (here).   You weren't . . . (plural)
In 1980 they were not (in Africa).   They weren't . . .

QUESTION FORM

Was I . . . ?
Were you . . . ?
   | he | | we |
Was | she | . . . ?   (singular) Were | you | . . . ? (plural)
   | it | | they |

Were you here yesterday?   **Were you** all in Rome then?
Was she in Africa in 1980?   **Were they** still alive in 1900?

be in the past simple can also be followed by an adjective, a noun, or a preposition plus noun (see ☞ 9.2.1).

9.2.3 *be* as an auxiliary verb (present continuous tense)

USE 3

We use **be** to form the PRESENT CONTINUOUS TENSE (11.1).
When **be, do** or **have** is used before a main verb to form a
tense, it is called an AUXILIARY VERB.

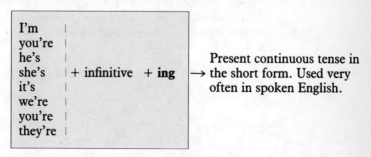

I'm	
you're	
he's	
she's	+ infinitive + **ing**
it's	
we're	
you're	
they're	

→ Present continuous tense in the short form. Used very often in spoken English.

I'm eating an apple at the moment.
She's waiting for an answer.

9.2.4 *be* as an auxiliary verb (past continuous tense)

USE 4

We use **be** to form the PAST CONTINUOUS TENSE (11.15):

I	was	
you	were	
he		
she	was	+ infinitive + **ing**
it		
we	were	
you	were	
they	were	

I was speaking when she entered the room.
He was lifting a box when he hurt his back.

 The verb **be** is also used in the formation of the PASSIVE (see
Chapter 17):

| (present simple) | ⟶ | **I am obliged** to pay. |
| (past simple) | ⟶ | **You were told** to go. |

9.3 Bird's eye box: be

I am late.	⟶ main verb, present simple
I was angry.	⟶ main verb, past simple
I am writing.	⟶ auxiliary verb, present continuous
I was writing.	⟶ auxiliary verb, past continuous
I am asked.	⟶ present passive
I was asked.	⟶ past passive

9.4 do

do . . . start?
don't start

doesn't like
don't think, do
do work, didn't
come, did

HANS: Hello, Miguel. What time **do** you **start** classes in your school? We **don't start** until 9.30.

MIGUEL: You're lucky! We start at 8.45 and the teacher **doesn't like** it if we are even a minute late! I **don't think** you **do** much work in your school.

HANS: Nonsense! We **do work**! I **didn't come** to England to waste my time. I even **did** an hour's homework on Saturday – before I went to the party!

form

POSITIVE			QUESTION			NEGATIVE (SHORT FORM)		
I	do	we do	Do	I?	Do we?	I	don't	we don't
you	do	you do	Do	you?	Do you?	you	don't	you don't
he				he?		he		
she	does	they do	Does	she?	Do they?	she	doesn't	they don't
it				it?		it		

9.4.1 *do* as an auxiliary verb (present simple tense)

USE 1 We use *do* as an AUXILIARY (9.2.3) to form the PRESENT SIMPLE TENSE (11.3) in questions and negative statements:

POSITIVE	NEGATIVE	QUESTION
I eat Indian food.	⟶ **I don't eat** Indian food.	⟶ **Do I eat** Indian food?
He eats Italian food	⟶ **He doesn't eat** Italian food.	⟶ **Does he eat** Italian food?
They eat Chinese food.	⟶ **They don't eat** Chinese food.	⟶ **Do they eat** Chinese food?

Written English uses the full form:

I **do not** eat.
He **does not** eat.

Spoken English uses the short form:

I **don't** eat.
He **doesn't** eat.
We **don't** like it.

The short form is used by English people when they speak to each other. It is a good idea to practise it in order to help you understand everyday conversation.

9.4.2 *do* as an auxiliary verb (past simple tense)

USE 2

did is used to form questions and negatives in the PAST SIMPLE TENSE (11.11–11.14):

POSITIVE	NEGATIVE (SHORT FORM)	QUESTION
I ate Russian food. ⟶	**I didn't eat** Russian food. ⟶	**Did I** really **eat** Russian food yesterday?
He spoke Italian. ⟶	**He didn't speak** Italian. ⟶	**Did he speak** Italian yesterday?
They tried hard. ⟶	**They didn't try** hard. ⟶	**Did they try** hard yesterday?

NOTE

In questions and negatives the main verb is always an INFINITIVE (9.1).

9.4.3 *do* as a main verb (present tenses)

USE 3

As a main verb **do** has the meaning 'to be busy/occupied with' something:

Women who have jobs often **do** their housework at weekends. They **are doing** their homework.
⟶ They are occupied with it.

In the summer the children **do** rock-climbing and fishing while we relax.
⟶ This is how they occupy/amuse themselves.

9.4.4 *do* as a main verb (past simple tense)

USE 4

POSITIVE	QUESTION	NEGATIVE (SHORT FORM)
I did my homework.	Did I do the right work?	I didn't do my homework.
You did your exercises.	Did you do the work?	You didn't do it.
He/she did his/her job.	Did|he|do the work? |she| |it|	He | She | didn't do enough. It |
It did all right.		
We did our best.	Did we do the right work?	We didn't do it.
You did the training.	Did you do the work?	You didn't do anything.
They did their washing.	Did they do the work?	They didn't do much.

What **did you do** last night?
I didn't do anything on Sunday, I was too tired.

9.4.5 *do* for emphasis

do, **does** and **did** are sometimes used to emphasize a statement, to express something strongly:

I **do** like this food, but I'm afraid I can't finish it.
I **did** want to come to the party but I was ill.
She *does* play tennis well!

9.4.6 *do* or *make*

These two verbs are often confused. In general, **do** is used for obligation or for something thought of as work:

Your must **do** your **homework**.
I'll **do** my **shopping** on Saturday.

make is used for actions which are more creative or which involve constructing something:

She's **making** her own **wedding dress**.
They've **made** their holiday **plans**.

Notice the difference between these two sentences:
I'm going to **make** a cake.
⟶ *create* a cake.
You do the cake and I'll **do** the sandwiches.
⟶ It's your *job* to *make* the cake.

NOTE

to make a bed means to put sheets, blankets, etc. on it.

9.5   Bird's eye box: do

> **Do** your homework immediately! ——→ obligation/work
>
> **I don't** understand.   ——→ auxiliary verb, present simple
> **Do I** understand?
>
> **I didn't** understand.   ——→ auxiliary verb, past simple
> **Did I** understand?
>
> **I do** the shopping on Saturdays. ——→ main verb, present simple
>
> **I did** my work yesterday. ——→ main verb, past simple
>
> I *do* love you! ——→ for emphasis

9.6   *have* as a main verb (present simple tense)

don't have have had didn't have has	I would like to live in Brazil but I **don't have** any idea how I can manage this. At the moment I **have** a job here in Europe and, of course, I've signed a contract so it's not so easy to move away. It might be a good idea to apply for some jobs over there. Last year, in fact, I **had** the opportunity to work in Rio de Janeiro but I **didn't have** the courage to go. I've also heard that Brazil **has** a lot of problems with inflation.

―――――― **form** ――――――

As a main verb: PRESENT SIMPLE TENSE (11.3)

POSITIVE ——→ SHORT FORM

I have (a chance).   I've (a good idea).
You have (a flat).   You've (a lovely smile).
He | He's ⎫
She | has (a bungalow).   She's ⎬ got (a good job).   ⎫ (singular)
It | It's got (a big garden).   ⎭

We have (a farm).   We've (time).   ⎫
You have (a boat).   You've (enough money).   ⎬ (plural)
They have (a garden).   They've (a house).   ⎭

QUESTION   NEGATIVE (SHORT FORM)
Do I have (a chance)?   I don't have (a chance).
Do you have (a flat)?   You don't have (a flat).   ⎫
    | he | He | ⎬ (singular)
Does | she | have (a house)? She | doesn't have (a house) ⎭
    | it | It |

Do we | | (a result)?   We don't have (a result).   ⎫
Do you | have | (a boat)?   You don't have (a boat).   ⎬ (plural)
Do they | | (a garden)?   They don't have (a garden). ⎭

NOTE

The contraction (short form) for **he has, she has** and **it has** is the same as for **he is, she is** and **it is**.
To avoid confusion, the contraction is usually formed with *got*:

He's a good boy.   He's (got) an interest in history.
⟶ He is . . .   ⟶ He has . . .

9.6.1   have/have got (possession)

USE 1

have as a main verb means 'possess' or 'own'. We use it generally to show that something belongs to us, that it is ours:

He **has** a motor bike.
⟶ The motor bike belongs to him. It is his motor bike.

John **has** a large house with a garden.
I **have** no spare time at the moment.
He **has** no idea what to do when he leaves school.

There is an alternative to this form of **have** when it means 'possess' or 'own' (see also ☞ below). This is very often used in spoken English:

I've got a headache.   **We've got** no plans.
You've got a big house.   **You've got** a big family.
He's ⎫
She's ⎭ got a new job.   **They've got** a good idea.

Questions and negatives are made like this:

A: **Have you got** a watch on?
B: No. I'm sorry. I **haven't got** any idea what the time is.

Remember this form is usually spoken; the stress is on **got**.

9.6.2   Other meanings of *have*

 In some special phrases **have** takes on a special meaning apart from 'possess':
John and Eric **are having an argument**.
⟶ John and Eric **are arguing**.
We **are having a party** on Saturday.
⟶ We **are holding** a party on Saturday.
Have a good time on your holidays.
⟶ **Enjoy yourself** on your holidays.
He **has a shower** twice a day.
⟶ He **takes a shower** twice a day.

In these situations the formation with **'ve got** can never be used.

9.6.3 *have* as a main verb (past simple tense)

USE 2

POSITIVE	QUESTION
I had a new bicycle.	Did I have a new bicycle?
You had a new bicycle.	Did you have a new bicycle?
He ⎫ had a new bicycle. She ⎭	Did ⎧ he ⎫ have a new bicycle? ⎩ she ⎭
It had red wheels.	Did it have red wheels?
We had a new car.	Did we have a new car?
You had a new car.	Did you have a new car?
They had a new car.	Did they have a new car?

NEGATIVE (SHORT FORM)	NEGATIVE (ALTERNATIVE SHORT FORM)
I didn't have a new bicycle.	
You didn't have a new bicycle.	I'd no idea.
He ⎫ didn't have a new bicycle. She ⎭	You'd no idea. He'd no idea.
It didn't have red wheels.	We'd no reason to ask.
We didn't have a new car.	
You didn't have a new car.	
They didn't have a new car.	

We had a good holiday although **we didn't have** a lot of money.

NOTE

When **had** means 'possessed' it can also be used with **got** in conversational English:

A: **Had you got** that hairstyle when I saw you last week?
B: **I had** the style, but **I hadn't got** the red colour!

9.6.4 *have* as an auxiliary verb (present/past perfect tenses)

USE 3

We use **have** as an AUXILIARY (9.2.3) to form other tenses:

PRESENT PERFECT	PAST PERFECT
I have been to the sea.	**I had** never **been** to the sea before I visited Cornwall.
We've often **been** there.	**He'd** never **been** there.
He has drunk the wine.	**He had drunk** the wine before I arrived.

91

See 11.17–11.18 for the PRESENT PERFECT TENSE and
11.22–11.23 for the PAST PERFECT TENSE.

9.7   Bird's eye box: have

I have a lot of friends. I've got a lot of friends.	⟶ main verb ('possess')
He has a shower every morning.	⟶ main verb (other meanings)
They had a swim in the sea every day last year.	⟶ main verb, past simple
I have ⎪ seen the film. I've ⎪	⟶ auxiliary verb, present perfect
I had ⎪ seen the film. I'd ⎪	⟶ auxiliary verb, past perfect

10 MODAL VERBS AND MODAL VERB PHRASES

IRREGULAR MODALS

10.1   Modal verbs and modal verb phrases: Introduction

must must, can will need to ought to 'd better, oughtn't to	POLICEMAN: OK. I've been following your car now for ten minutes. You've been driving at far more than the speed limit and in a very erratic manner. I think you **must** have had a little too much to drink. DRIVER: I really **must** protest, officer. I **can** assure you that I only drank one glass of whisky – or maybe two. POLICEMAN: **Will** you show me your driving licence? And I **need to** check your insurance papers too. DRIVER: Er . . . I haven't got them with me. I know that I **ought to** keep them in the car but I always forget. POLICEMAN: I think you forgot to stop drinking too! You**'d better** get into my car. You certainly **oughtn't to** drive any further tonight.

——————— **form** ———————

MODAL VERBS

will *or* 'll★ shall *or* 'll★ would *or* 'd can could should ought to† may might	+ main verb infinitive (9.1)	must have to† need (to)† used to† dare (to)†	+ main verb infinitive

★See ☞ 1.   †See ☞ 2.

94

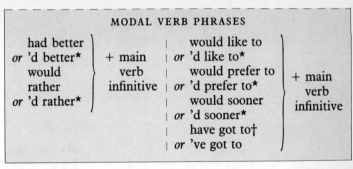

```
                    MODAL VERB PHRASES
    had better  ⎫                   │   would like to
or 'd better*   ⎪   + main          │ or 'd like to*
    would       ⎬     verb          │   would prefer to    ⎫   + main
    rather      ⎪   infinitive      │ or 'd prefer to*     ⎬     verb
or 'd rather*   ⎭                   │   would sooner        ⎪   infinitive
                                    │ or 'd sooner*         ⎭
                                    │   have got to†
                                    │ or 've got to
```

*See ☞ 1.

1 In the form box above we see that some modal verbs have a short form (*). This is often used in spoken English. The full form is always used in formal written English (for example, in a business letter).

USE | **Expressing an attitude to an action/state**

1   Modal verbs (and modal verb phrases) are different from other verbs because: they do not normally stand alone. They are nearly always used in front of a main verb. The main verb is always an INFINITIVE (9.1).

The modal verb changes the attitude or mood of the main verb:

I **must leave** you now.
They **might be** on this train.
She **ought to know** the answer.

Modal verbs help us to show a different attitude to the main action verb:

I **must**   speak. ⟶ strong obligation
I **ought to** speak. ⟶ moral obligation
I **might**   speak. ⟶ slight possibility

2   When we want to make a question with modals we change the word order:

```
1     2    3              2    1   3
We must learn. ⟶ Must we learn?
2     1   3                        2   1 3
Must we learn all these silly rules?   Can I go swimming now?
```

> **3** When we want to make a negative we put **not** after
> the modal verb. In spoken English **not** usually
> becomes **n't**:

I **can** speak.   ⟶   I **cannot** speak.
or
I **can't** speak.

He **could** learn.   ⟶   He **could not** learn.
or
He **couldn't** learn.

They **ought to** pay.   ⟶   They **ought not to** pay.
or
They **oughtn't to** pay.

 2 **ought to, have to, have got to, need to, used to, dare to**
are not true modal verbs. See IRREGULAR MODALS
(10.25–10.30).

REGULAR MODALS

10.2   will (future – 'willingness to')

> *In the Manager's office*
>
> SALESMAN: I'd like to see you for a minute, sir, if you've
> time. I've got a bit of a problem.
>
> *won't, 'll*   MANAGER: Certainly. **I won't** be a moment, **I'll** just ask
> *'ll*   my secretary to take incoming calls and then **I'll** help
> you if I can.
>
> ────── **form** ──────
>
> POSITIVE (SHORT FORM)   POSITIVE (LONG FORM)
>
> **'ll** + infinitive   **will** + infinitive
>
> NEGATIVE (SHORT FORM)   NEGATIVE (LONG FORM)
>
> **won't** + infinitive   **will not** + infinitive
>
> QUESTION
>
> will (**I**, etc.) + infinitive?

<table>
<tr><td>

USE
</td><td>

Willingness to do something in the future

(See WILL (FUTURE) 11.27).

will has several meanings, all of them connected with the future. Here it means 'willing to':

I'll help you if I can.
⟶ I am willing to help you.
</td></tr>
</table>

10.2.1 will (offers/emphasis)

	Mrs Smith is visiting Mrs Jones at home
will . . . ?	MRS SMITH: It's so nice to see you, Mrs Jones. **Will** you take a seat while I fetch the tea-tray?
	MRS JONES: Thank you. What a lovely room.
will . . . ?	MRS SMITH: First of all, Mrs Jones, **will** you have a piece of chocolate cake?
	MRS JONES: That's a wonderful idea. I won't refuse today but I will go on a diet next week.

USE 1

Offers

This is a special use of **will** + infinitive. We use it to make an offer to somebody:

Will you have a sandwich?
⟶ I want to offer you a sandwich.
Will you drink a coffee or a cup of tea?
⟶ Do you want a coffee or a cup of tea?

USE 2

Emphasis

Will (in full form only) is sometimes used to stress, or emphasize, a point:

TEENAGE DAUGHTER (*to mother*): I **will** go out with my hair like this if I want to.

10.3 Bird's eye box: will

I'll do it.	⟶ I'm willing to do it.
Will you have some cake?	⟶ Would you like some cake?
I *will* be heard.	⟶ emphasis

10.4 shall . . . ?

shall . . . ?

shall . . . ?
shall . . . ?

> JIM: I fancy going to the cinema this evening for a
> change. What do you think? **Shall** we go?
> ROBERT: We could. What's on?
> JIM: There's a James Bond film on.
> ROBERT: OK. **Shall** I call for you? We could go by car.
> **Shall** I pick you up at about 6 o'clock?
> JIM: Thanks very much. That'd be great.
>
> ——————————— **form** ———————————
>
> **shall I/we** + infinitive?

USE 1

Offering help – polite

We ask questions using **shall** to offer help:

Shall I do it for you?
⟶ Would you like me to do it for you?

Shall I pick you up from the station?
⟶ Would you like me to pick you up from the station?

shall . . . ? can only be used with **I** and **we**.

USE 2

Making a suggestion

We also ask questions using **shall** to make suggestions:

Shall we meet at your house?
⟶ I suggest we meet at your house.

Shall we go to the cinema?
⟶ Why don't we go to the cinema?

10.5 Bird's eye box: shall . . . ?

Shall I fetch you?	⟶	polite offer of help
Shall we have a picnic?	⟶	suggestion

10.6 would like to

'd like to

would . . .
like to . . . ?

'd like to
'd like to

> CLIENT: Well, I'd **like to** thank you for inviting me for a meal like this. It's really nice.
> BUSINESSMAN: It's all part of the service. What **would** you **like to** drink first?
> CLIENT: Well, I fancy a Martini to begin with.
> BUSINESSMAN: OK. I'd **like to** drink a tomato juice. Waiter! We'd **like to** see the menu, please.

form

POSITIVE (SHORT FORM)	POSITIVE (LONG FORM)
'd like to + infinitive	**would like to** + infinitive

NEGATIVE (SHORT FORM)
wouldn't like to + infinitive

NEGATIVE (LONG FORM)
would not like to + infinitive

QUESTION
would (you, etc.**) like to** + infinitive?

USE

More polite than 'want to'

We use **would like to** when we want to say that something would give us pleasure. It is a more polite form than **want to**:

> ARTHUR: What **would you like to do** this evening, Jenny?
> JENNY: **I'd like to stay** in really.

or

> ARTHUR: What**'d you like to eat** today, Jenny?
> JENNY: Oh, I want to try an Indian meal this evening.

10.6.1 would prefer to/would sooner/would rather

would . . .
rather . . . ?
'd . . . prefer to

'd sooner

> JACKIE: Let's plan our summer holiday. Where **would** you **rather** go this year? Spain or Italy?
> JEFF: Well, **I'd** really **prefer to** have an active holiday for a change – maybe walking in Switzerland or even canoeing in Scotland.
> JACKIE: If those are your only suggestions, **I'd sooner** stay at home! Come on – be reasonable. I'm not athletic and I need two weeks' sun every year!
> JEFF: OK. Calm down. We'll do whatever you prefer. We usually do!

---

form

POSITIVE (SHORT FORM)	POSITIVE (LONG FORM)
'd prefer to |	| **prefer to** |
'd sooner | + infinitive	**would** | **sooner** | + infinitive
'd rather |	| **rather** |

NEGATIVE (SHORT FORM)	NEGATIVE (LONG FORM)
'd prefer not to |	| **prefer not to** |
'd sooner not | + infinitive	**would** | **sooner not** | + infinitive
'd rather not |	| **rather not** |

QUESTION

would (**you**, etc.) | **prefer to** \|
| **sooner** \| + infinitive
| **rather** \|

USE

Choosing something from several alternatives

I'd prefer to = I'd rather = I'd sooner
These phrases show that the speaker wants to choose
something from several alternatives:

'Which of the television sets
would you like if you could
choose?'

'**I'd prefer to take** this one.'
(*or*
I'd sooner take this one.
I'd rather take this one.)
'It's the biggest!'

Connectors

(See LINKING WORDS, Chapter 23)
Joan **would prefer to** get on with her work **than** to go to the
party.
He**'d rather** spend his evenings alone **than** mix with other
people.
They**'d rather** enjoy themselves while they are young **than** wait
until they are old.

Would you rather drink tea **or** coffee?
Would you sooner spend an evening watching television **or** playing darts?

NOTE

1 **than** is used in statements and **or** in questions.
2 The negative form uses **not** and not **n't**:
    I'd sooner **not** come, if you don't mind.
See also SECOND CONDITIONAL, 19.2.

10.7 Bird's eye box: would

> **I'd like to** go soon. (more polite) ⟶ I want to go soon.
>
> **I'd prefer to** ⟶ **I'd sooner** ⟶ **I'd rather** leave now.

10.8 should

should

should

shouldn't

MOTHER: Kathryn, I've been wanting to talk to you about something. Have you got a minute?
KATHRYN: OK. What's the problem now?
MOTHER: You know you don't have a job and you're getting money from the Social Security. You said you wanted to prepare for your exams. I think you **should** stay at home and do some work.
KATHRYN: And I think you **should** leave me alone. You don't know if I'm working or not. It's not your business.
MOTHER: Kathryn! You **shouldn't** talk to me like that! I'm your mother.

─── form ───

POSITIVE

should + infinitive

NEGATIVE (SHORT FORM)

shouldn't + infinitive

NEGATIVE (LONG FORM)

should not + infinitive

QUESTION

should (**I**, etc.) + infinitive?

USE

Moral obligation

Should is used to tell somebody that they have a moral obligation to do something. It is often used when one person gives very strong advice to another:

You shouldn't smoke so much.

You look tired. **You should go** to bed earlier.

You shouldn't throw litter on the street. **You should put** it in the litter bin.

10.9 ought to

TRAINER: OK, boys. We've got the big competition in front of us now. It's our big chance. You must train harder than ever.

ought to

PLAYER: We're going to do that. You needn't worry. But I think we **ought to** practise more often together this week.

oughtn't to

COACH: No, we **oughtn't to** overdo it. We'll become stale and tired. We shouldn't risk that.

──── **form** ────

POSITIVE

ought to + infinitive

NEGATIVE (SHORT FORM)

oughtn't to + infinitive

NEGATIVE (LONG FORM)
ought not to + infinitive

QUESTION
ought (**I**, etc.) **to** + infinitive?

Moral obligation

See also **should**, 10.8.

You **ought to give up** smoking if it makes you cough.
You **oughtn't to drive** a car if you have drunk alcohol.

In most cases **ought to** means much the same as **should**:

He **should clean** his car. It's a disgrace.
or
He **ought to clean** his car. It's a disgrace.

Both sentences express the belief that he has a duty, a moral obligation, to clean his car.

ought to often seems rather stronger and more impersonal:

Young children **oughtn't to** watch too much TV.
——→ impersonal statement
You've watched enough TV, you **should** go to bed now.
——→ direct personal statement

10.10 Bird's eye box: should/ought to

> I **should finish** this work ——→ I **ought to finish** this work.
> ——→ It would be better for me to finish this work.

10.11 can (ability)

can   ETHNE: It's really great here in this lake. The water's so warm. And it's so clean. I **can** see the bottom. It's quite deep.

can   DAVID: Ethne! Be careful. I know you **can** swim but you shouldn't swim out too far in such cold water.

can   ETHNE: Don't worry about me. I **can** swim for miles without getting tired.

can't
can't   DAVID: All right then, but I'm getting out. I **can't** swim as fast as you and I **can't** stand being beaten by a girl!

— **form** —

POSITIVE
can + infinitive

NEGATIVE (SHORT FORM)   NEGATIVE (LONG FORM)
can't + infinitive   **cannot** + infinitive

QUESTION
can (**you**, etc.) + infinitive?

USE

Present ability

We use **can** + infinitive to say that we are able to do something. It is in our power to do it:

I can see you.
⟶ I am able to see you.

She can swim.
⟶ She is able to swim. She knows how to swim.

1 Future ability

We have two ways of expressing ability to do something in the future:

Tomorrow I **can** go to the beach. Next week we **can** buy a new car.	*or* Tomorrow **I'll be able to** go to the beach. Next week we**'ll be able to** buy a new car.

2 could – past ability

When we want to say that we had the ability to do something in the past we use **was/were able to** or **could**:

Pauline **could** speak better Italian when she was at school, but now she has forgotten a lot.

Last year **I could run** a mile in 4 minutes.
or
Last year **I was able to run** a mile in 4 minutes.

Now I can run a mile – but I need 15 minutes!
or
Now **I'm able to run** a mile – but I need 15 minutes!

PAST TIME   PRESENT TIME

DANGER   **could** is not always the past of **can**. In some situations it has other meanings or uses (see **could** 10.13–10.14).

10.11.1 can (permission)

can . . . ?

can't

can

> DRIVER: Excuse me. **Can** I park here for five minutes while I wait for a friend?
>
> TRAFFIC WARDEN: No, I'm afraid you **can't**. These double yellow lines mean that no parking is allowed. But if you drive round the corner you **can** park there for thirty minutes without any problems.

USE

Present permission

Can I park? = May I park?

In the past **may** was very often used to ask for permission and is still considered very polite, but **can** is now much more common:

You can go home now.
Can I possibly **be excused** from this meeting?
Can I have another cup of tea?
They can leave as soon as they want.

1 Future permission

You can **come** again **tomorrow**.

The class **can** leave early on **Friday** afternoon because there is a trip to London.
⟶ The class has permission to leave early.

2 Could – past permission

When we want to talk about permission given in the past we use **could**:

When I **was** a child I **couldn't** choose what I ate, but **now** I **can**.

NOTE

As **could** has several meanings (10.13–10.14) it is sometimes clearer to use **allowed to** when talking about permission given in the past:

Last year I **wasn't allowed to** drive because the police took my licence away.

DANGER

could is not always the past of **can**. In some situations it has other meanings or uses (see **could** 10.13–10.14).

10.12 Bird's eye box: can

I can see for miles.	⟶	present ability
I can come with you tomorrow.	⟶	future ability
I could see more clearly when I was younger.	⟶	past ability
Can we drive more than forty miles an hour here?	⟶	present permission
Can I borrow your car next week?	⟶	future permission
When he was a policeman he **could/was allowed to** break the speed limit.	⟶	past permission

10.13 could . . . ?

could . . . ?

could . . . ?

could . . . ?

JOHNNY: Excuse me, sir. It's cold in this classroom. **Could** I close the window?

TEACHER: OK, Johnny. Close it quickly and then sit down and get on with the test.

JOHNNY: Sir, **could** I have another sheet of paper? I've spoiled this one.

TEACHER: Here's another sheet. Now, please get on with your work.

JOHNNY: Sir! Sir! **Could** I just leave the room for a few minutes?

TEACHER: Why didn't you go before you began the exam?

JOHNNY: I didn't want to go then, sir.

————— **form** —————

could (I, etc.) + infinitive?

USE

Requests

We use **could . . . ?** when we want somebody to do something for us or to allow us to do something. We make a request:

POLICEMAN: **Could I have** your name and address, please?
DRIVER: It's James Ford, 6 Old Village Road, Durham.

Could you open the window? It's so hot in this room.

10.13.1 could

could

could

could

could

> MARIA: Why don't we take a trip to Cornwall this
>   weekend?
> SARAH: I'd love to, but Sam **could** be coming for a few
>   days. Could we all go together?
> MARIA: Yes, I should think so. Perhaps Jack **could** come
>   too.
> SARAH: Yes, good idea. Do you think we **could** book
>   rooms at a hotel so late in the season?
> MARIA: Well, we can try. I must go now. I can hear
>   noises outside. It **could** be my boss. 'Bye.

――――――――― **form** ―――――――――

POSITIVE

could + infinitive

NEGATIVE (SHORT FORM)   NEGATIVE (LONG FORM)

couldn't + infinitive   **could not** + infinitive

QUESTION

could II, etc.) + infinitive?

I must go now. I can hear noises outside. **It could be** my boss.

| USE |

Possibility

We use **could** when we want to talk about the possibility of
something happening. We are not sure or certain about the
situation:

She could visit her sister.

⟶ She **might** (10.17) /**may** (10.15.1) visit her sister. It is possible she will visit her.

Kathryn could pass her exam next week.

⟶ It is possible she will pass but we cannot say for certain. We are not sure.

Be careful! **Somebody could come** around the corner at any minute.

See ⟶ **could** in INDIRECT SPEECH (20.2, 20.3 ☞ 3).

10.14 Bird's eye box: could . . . ?/could

Could you **give** me a light, please?	⟶	request
Next year I **could give up** my job and retire.	⟶	possibility

10.15 may (permission)

	CUSTOMER: I'd like to join the library.
	LIBRARIAN: Could you fill this form in, please.
may . . . ?	CUSTOMER: All right. How many books **may** I take out?
	LIBRARIAN: You can have up to five books for two
may	weeks. You **may** keep them longer but you must renew them first.
may . . . ?	CUSTOMER: **May** I take five books with me today, straight away?
	LIBRARIAN: Yes, of course.

─────────────── **form** ───────────────

POSITIVE	NEGATIVE
may + infinitive	**may not** + infinitive

QUESTION

may (**I**, etc.) + infinitive?

but

may you . . . ?

 We do not use a short form of **may not** in modern English.

USE

More formal than can/could . . . ?

We use **may** when we want to ask or give permission:

May I leave the room?
⟶ Can I leave the room?
⟶ Could I please leave the room?

may is rather formal and sounds a little old-fashioned. It is certainly very polite:

You may wait in my office but **you may not smoke**.
May Paul bring a friend with him to my party?
May I wear jeans and a sweater?

Most often we use **can** (10.11.1) or **could** . . . ? (10.13)

10.15.1 may (possibility)

USE

Present/future possibility

We use **may** when we want to show we are uncertain about something. We could be speaking about the future:

I may come to your party **tomorrow**, but I'm not sure. **I may go** to London for the weekend instead.

or about the present (although it is more common to use **perhaps** in this case):

The teacher may have my book. I hope so.
⟶ **Perhaps** the teacher has my book.

 We can also use **might** (10.17) instead of **may**:

We **may** play squash this evening if we have time.
or
We **might** play squash this evening if we have time.

might is a little less certain.

See also **could** (10.13.1).

10.16 Bird's eye box: may

May I **come** an hour later?	⟶ permission
She **may have** the money. I don't know.	⟶ possibility

10.17   might

might

mightn't

might

> PETER: Are we going out tonight or shall we stay in?
> LIZ: I think I'd prefer to stay at home. I **might** cook a tasty meal. What do you fancy?
> PETER: Well, we can't have anything too grand. We **mightn't** have enough cash to buy the ingredients.
> LIZ: All right. Let's make spaghetti. That's cheap enough.
> PETER: I'm looking forward to this. I **might** even help you if you're lucky!

---

form

POSITIVE

might + infinitive

NEGATIVE (SHORT FORM)   NEGATIVE (LONG FORM)

mightn't + infinitive   **might not** + infinitive

QUESTION

might (I, etc.) + infinitive?

USE

Possibility

might means almost the same as **could** (10.13.1) and **may** (POSSIBILITY 10.15.1)). It shows that we are not quite as certain as when we use **could** or **may:**

Jane **could** arrive at 6 o'clock.	⟶	possible
Jane **may** arrive at 6 o'clock.	⟶	fairly possible
Jane **might** arrive at 6 o'clock.	⟶	possible, but unlikely

 We often finish **might** sentences with **but I doubt it/but I don't think so.** This expresses even more uncertainty:

The sun **might** shine today, **but I doubt it.**

10.18   Bird's eye box: might

I **might have** my holiday in August.	⟶	unlikely possibility

10.19   must/have to

At the embassy

have to — CUSTOMER: I wonder if you can tell me what the special requirements are for a visit to Poland?
must — OFFICIAL: First you **have to** arrange a visa. This can take up to three weeks so you **must** apply early.
'll have to — CUSTOMER: Thank you. I**'ll have to** contact my friend before I can make any definite arrangements. But I can
'll have to — see we**'ll have to** move quickly if we want to travel in July.
must — OFFICIAL: Yes, sir. You **must** fill in the form as soon as you can.

———— **form** ————

POSITIVE	NEGATIVE
must + infinitive	(see ☞ 2 and 3)
have to + infinitive	

QUESTION
(see ☞ 4)

USE

Obligation/compulsion

I must and **I have to** both mean 'I am obliged to', 'I am compelled to'.

The difference between **must** and **have to** is slight. **must** suggests the obligation comes from you, the speaker:

I must get my hair cut.
———→ I feel the obligation. It is self-imposed.

You mustn't speak to me like that.
———→ direct obligation from speaker to listener.

have to suggests obligation from a third person, often a higher authority:

The **boss** says **we have to work** until 7 o'clock.

The **policeman** said **I have to take** my driving licence to the police station.

 1   have got to ——→ 've got to

Like **have to,** this term suggests that another person has told us to do something. In everyday language we use **have ('ve) got to** very often:

I must ⟶ I have to ⟶ I've got to

David **must** work late this evening.
or
David **has to** work late this evening.
or
David **has got to** work late this evening.
David**'s got to** work late this evening.
(informal/spoken English)

2 Negative forms of **must/have to**

I don't have to = I haven't got to

I don't have to pay for the meal.
or
I haven't got to pay for the meal.
⟶ It's not necessary for me to pay for the meal.

I'm not working today so **I haven't got to** get up early.
⟶ I'm not working today so it isn't necessary to get up early.

DANGER | **I mustn't** means 'I am not allowed to', 'I am forbidden to'.

You mustn't cross the road when the traffic lights **are** red.
⟶ You aren't allowed to cross the road when the traffic lights are red.

Children mustn't speak with their mouths full.

3 We can use an alternative form for **haven't (got) to** and **don't have to**:

I **don't need to** speak.
You **don't need to** come.

See **need to** (10.25).

 4 Questions with **must** and **have to**:

A   B

Must I	(speak)?
Must you	(leave)?
Must he	(drive)?
Must they	(come)?

Have I	(got) to (speak)?
Have you	(got) to (leave)?
Has he	(got) to (drive)?
Have they	(got) to (come)?

C

Do I	have to (speak)?
Do you	have to (leave)?
Does he	have to (drive)?
Do they	have to (come)?

The forms A, B and C above all generally have the meaning 'Is it necessary for (me, etc.) to (speak, etc.)?'

Must he drive so fast?
= **Has he (got) to** drive so fast?
= **Does he have to** drive so fast?

10.20 Bird's eye box: must/have to

I **must leave** at 6 o'clock. ⎫ I **have to leave** at 6 o'clock. ⎬ ⟶ I've **got to leave** at 6 o'clock. ⎭	I'm obliged to leave at 6 o'clock
I **mustn't drive**. ⟶ I'm not allowed to drive.	
I **don't have to drive**. ⎫ I **haven't (got) to drive**. ⎬ ⟶ I **don't need to drive**. ⎭	It's not necessary for me to drive.

10.21   must (logicality/certainty)

must

must
must have

must

> JOHN: Where do you live?
> RITA: In Elm Grove – at number 6.
> JOHN: Really! That **must** be next door to my friend Malcolm.
> RITA: Oh, I don't think I know him.
> JOHN: You **must** know him! He's a fanatical runner. You **must have** seen him running round your area in all weathers.
> RITA: Oh! you **must** mean the man with the red bicycle! Yes, I've seen him but I didn't know he was a friend of yours.

USE

must in the text above has a different meaning from that in **must/have to** (10.19). Here John and Rita use **must** when they want to say, 'It's certain or logical that . . .'

I spoke to you for 45 minutes yesterday. **You must remember me.**
⟶ I spoke to you for 45 minutes yesterday so it's logical or certain that you remember me. (I deduce it.)

☞ With this usage of **must** the negative is **cannot** or **can't**:

POSITIVE		NEGATIVE
You **must** know the answer.	⟶	You **can't** know the answer.
She **must** be 18.	⟶	She **can't** be 18.

10.22   Bird's eye box: must

> You **must** be very healthy after so much jogging.   logicality⟶certainty

10.23   had better

> CHRIS: Mell! I was digging in the garden and I've just
> cut my foot with the spade.
> MELL: Oh dear! How did you manage to do that? OK.
> 'd better   You'd **better** let me have a look.
> CHRIS: Ouch! It really hurts a lot.
> 'd better   MELL: It doesn't look too good. I think you'd **better** go
> along to the Out-patients Department at the hospital.
> 'd better   You'd **better** have an injection. There could be germs
> in the wound.

---

form

POSITIVE (SHORT FORM)	POSITIVE (LONG FORM)
'd better + infinitive	**had better** + infinitive

NEGATIVE (SHORT FORM)	NEGATIVE (LONG FORM)
'd better not + infinitive	**had better not** + infinitive

QUESTION

had (I, etc.) **better** + infinitive?

USE

Giving advice

I'd better means 'It would be better for me to', 'I should'.

We use **'d better** when we want to give somebody advice. We can also give advice to ourselves:

I'd better lose some weight.
She'd better save some money if she wants to go on holiday.
They'd better get some insurance for their house.

The meaning of **'d better** is similar to **should** (10.8) and **ought to** (10.9).

 1   **'d better** is the short form of **had better**, but we rarely use the full form in spoken English.

 2   We often ask questions in the negative form:

Hadn't you better phone your grandmother?
⟶ You should phone your grandmother.

10.24 Bird's eye box: had better

I'd better leave now.	⟶ It would be better for me to leave now.
Hadn't you **better** leave?	⟶ I think you should leave.

IRREGULAR MODALS

10.25 need (to)

At the driving school

need . . . ?   JEFF: I'd like to learn to drive. Could you explain to me what I have to do? For instance, **need** I own a car before I can start?

don't need to   INSTRUCTOR: No, you certainly **don't need to** have a car. In fact, we prefer to use our own cars as they have dual controls.

do... need to...?   JEFF: **Do** I **need to** do a written test as well as a practical one?

need to   INSTRUCTOR: No, but you **need to** know your highway code in detail.

need   JEFF: So all I really **need** now is the money for a course of lessons – and my courage!

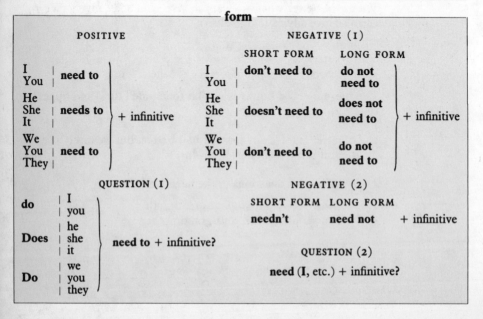

------ **form** ------

POSITIVE		NEGATIVE (1)		
			SHORT FORM	LONG FORM
I / You	**need to**	I / You	**don't need to**	**do not need to**
He / She / It	**needs to**	He / She / It	**doesn't need to**	**does not need to**
We / You / They	**need to**	We / You / They	**don't need to**	**do not need to**

(POSITIVE) + infinitive

(NEGATIVE (1)) + infinitive

QUESTION (1)			NEGATIVE (2)	
do	I / you		SHORT FORM	LONG FORM
Does	he / she / it	**need to** + infinitive?	**needn't**	**need not** + infinitive
Do	we / you / they			

QUESTION (2)

need (**I**, etc.) + infinitive?

USE

Necessity

I need to means 'It is necessary for me to'.

He needs to save money for his holiday.
⟶ It is necessary for him to save money for his holiday.

Does he need to arrange a visa?
⟶ Is it necessary for him to arrange a visa?

The meaning is very similar to **have to** (10.19.☞2).

1 Main verb or modal

In the present tense negative statements and questions take two forms:

1 need + to behaves as a regular main verb, making negatives with **don't/doesn't** and questions with **do/does**:

I **don't need to** go.   **Does** he **need to** go?

2 need without **to** behaves as a modal verb, making negatives with **not/n't** and questions by changing the word order:

I **needn't** go.   Need I go?

There is no great difference between the meanings of **1** and **2**.

NOTE

When **need** is used as a modal verb there is no **to** before the infinitive.

In positive statements in the present, **need** is always used like a main verb with **to**:

I **need to** go to the bank.

In tenses other than the present **need (to)** is used like a main verb:

I **didn't need to** ask him for the money.
Did you **need** a passport to go to Scotland?
You **won't need to** take a coat.

10.26 Bird's eye box: need (to)

+ **I need to** pay.	→ It's necessary for me to pay.
− **I don't need to** pay.	→ It's not necessary for me to pay.
− **I needn't** pay.	→ It's not necessary for me to pay.
? **Do I need to** pay?	→ Is it necessary for me to pay?
? **Need I** pay?	→ Is it necessary for me to pay?

10.27   used to

used to

did... use to...?

used to

> OLD JIM: We had a hard life. When I was a boy – eight years old – I **used to** work for a few pennies. I made tea for the coalminers here in Derbyshire.
> GRANDSON: How many hours **did** you **use to** work at the weekend, Grandad?
> OLD JIM: Well, we were busy from six o'clock on Saturday morning until eleven on Sunday evening. We **used to** stay in the mines for thirty-six hours at the weekend.
> GRANDSON: That was a long time, Grandad!

—— **form** ——

POSITIVE

used to + infinitive

NEGATIVE (SHORT FORM)	NEGATIVE (LONG FORM)
didn't use to + infinitive	**did not use to** + infinitive

QUESTION

did (I, etc.**) use to** + infinitive?

USE

Past habit

I used to means 'I did regularly in the past but now I have stopped'. The action described was a habit before, but now it has finished:

Contrast

PAST SIMPLE (11.11–11.14)		used to
Ten years ago I **was a** clerk.	⟶	Ten years ago I **used to be** a clerk.
Two years ago I **smoked** twenty cigarettes a day.	⟶	Two years ago I **used to smoke** twenty cigarettes a day.

would

An expression with a similar meaning to **used to** is **would**.

When we were young, my friends and I **would** walk along the beach for miles and miles.
⟶ We **used to** walk for miles.
⟶ We **walked** for miles.

10.28   Bird's eye box: used to

I **used to** play.	⟶ I very often played.
We **used to** know.	⟶ We knew.
I **didn't use to** pay.	⟶ I didn't usually pay.
Did you **use to** pay?	⟶ Did you pay?
We **would** play for hours.	⟶ We very often played for hours.

10.29   dare (to)

daren't

dare to

do . . . dare . . . ?

PETER: I've just failed all my exams. I **daren't** tell my father.

JAKE: I'm not surprised. I don't think I'd even **dare to** go home.

PETER: Well, in that case, I won't. I'll go to France and find a job there. **Do** you **dare** to come with me?

JAKE: Why not? It could be fun.

─────── **form** ───────

POSITIVE

I You	dare (to)	
He She It	dares (to)	+ infinitive
We You They	dare (to)	

119

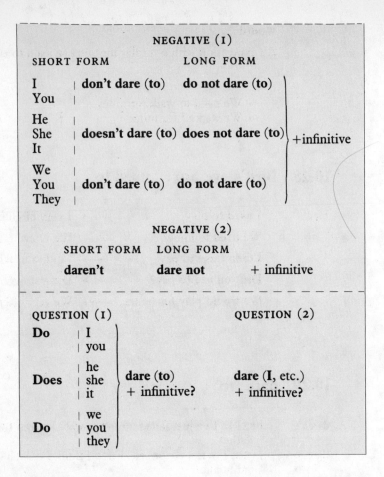

NEGATIVE (1)

SHORT FORM	LONG FORM	
I You	don't dare (to)	do not dare (to)
He She It	doesn't dare (to)	does not dare (to)
We You They	don't dare (to)	do not dare (to)

+infinitive

NEGATIVE (2)

SHORT FORM	LONG FORM	
daren't	dare not	+ infinitive

QUESTION (1)			QUESTION (2)
Do	I you		
Does	he she it	dare (to) + infinitive?	dare (I, etc.) + infinitive?
Do	we you they		

USE

'have the courage to'

dare (to) means 'have the courage to' and is usually found in the negative:

I daren't look at the gas bill, I'm sure it's enormous.

Don't you dare try to walk across the road until the light is green!

1 dare (to) has two forms like **need (to)** (10.25).

I **don't dare (to)** do it. (1) ⎱
I **daren't** do it. (2) ⎰
⟶ I haven't the courage to do it.

Do I **dare (to)** do it? (1) ⎱
Dare I do it? (2) ⎰
⟶ Have I the courage to do it?

 2 I daresay

This has a special meaning: 'It seems likely or possible (that)'.

I daresay it'll rain if we decide to have a picnic.

We only use this expression in positive statements.

10.30 Bird's eye box: dare (to)

+ **I dare (to)** speak.	⟶ I have the courage to speak.
− **I don't dare (to)** speak.	⟶ I'm afraid to speak.
− **I daren't** speak.	⟶ I'm afraid to speak.
? **Do I dare (to)** speak?	⟶ Have I the courage to speak?
? **Dare I** speak?	⟶ Have I the courage to speak?
+ **I daresay** you know him.	⟶ It seems very possible (that) you know him.

11 TENSES OF THE VERB (ACTIVE)

CONTENTS

11.1 Present continuous (formation)

What are they doing now?

is doing
is watching, is
reading, is playing
are . . . feeling

In the picture John **is doing** his homework at a table. Mrs Smith **is watching** television and Mr Smith **is reading** the paper. Sam **is playing** with a car and they **are** all **feeling** very relaxed.

─── **form** ───

POSITIVE   → SHORT FORM

present simple + present participle   + (other information)
   of **be**   (infinitive   + **ing**)

					SHORT FORM
I	am	eat____ing	(an apple).		I'm eating . . .
You	are	drink____ing	(a cocktail).		You're drinking . . .
He					He's
She	is	wait____ing	(at the station).		She's waiting . . .
It					It's
We					We're
You	are	try____ing	(hard).		You're trying . . .
They					They're

NEGATIVE   → SHORT FORM (1)   SHORT FORM (2)

present + **not** + present
simple of   participle . . .
  be

				SHORT FORM (1)	SHORT FORM (2)
I	am	not	eating . . .	—	I'm not eating . . .
You	are	not	drinking . . .	You aren't drinking...	You're not drinking...
He				He	He's
She	is	not	waiting . . .	She isn't waiting . . .	She's not waiting . . .
It				It	It's
We				We	We're
You	are	not	trying . . .	You aren't trying. . .	You're not trying . . .
They				They	They're

QUESTION

present simple + present participle . . . ?
   of **be**

Am	I	eating . . . ?	
Are	you	drinking . . . ?	
	he		
Is	she	waiting . . . ?	
	it		
	we		
Are	you	trying . . . ?	
	they		

 1 When we speak we use the short form of this tense:

   I am speaking. ⟶ **I'm** speaking.
   You are not reading. ⟶ **You aren't** reading.

NOTE

The short form of **I am not** is **I'm not**. There is no short form for questions.

It is also possible to use the complete form when we speak. We do this when we want to emphasize the fact that an action is happening:

PETER: John, you're not trying. Push harder!
JOHN: Just be quiet! I *am* trying.
⟶ I'm really trying.

2 Spelling present participles

1 When the verb infinitive ends with **e** we leave this off when we add **ing**:

drive ⟶ I am **driving**.
jok**e** ⟶ He is **joking**.

2 When a verb has only one syllable and ends with a vowel (a, e, i, o, u) followed by a single CONSONANT (3.6.) ☞ the consonant is doubled before **ing** (see table below).

3 The final consonant is doubled in longer verbs when the vowel before it is single and stressed in pronunciation:

per**mit** ⟶ per**mitting** *but* bloss**om** ⟶ bloss**oming**

However the letter **y** is never doubled:

re**pay** ⟶ re**paying**   em**ploy** ⟶ em**ploying**

2		3	
cut	⟶ cutting	regret	⟶ regretting
get	⟶ getting	prefer	⟶ preferring
swim	⟶ swimming	begin	⟶ beginning
clap	⟶ clapping	forbid	⟶ forbidding
dig	⟶ digging	fulfil	⟶ fulfilling
run	⟶ running		

4 When the basic verb ends with **ie** this becomes **y** in the **ing** form:

d**ie** ⟶ d**ying**   l**ie** ⟶ l**ying**.

These rules apply in the formation of other tenses, GERUNDS (see Chapter 15), and PARTICIPLES (see Chapter 16).

11.1.1 Present continuous (use)

We use the PRESENT CONTINUOUS when an action is happening *at this moment, now* (at the time of speaking or writing). We often use words (adverbs or adverbial phrases) with the present continuous which tell us that the action is happening now:

now	at the moment	at present	(at) this minute
right now	just now		

He's eating an apple.

PAST TIME	NOW	FUTURE TIME

At the moment she's playing the piano in the other room.
Right now he's sitting in his car.

11.1.2 Present continuous with *always*

're always leaving

're always
complaining

're forever telling

> WIFE: Oh, don't put your coat on that chair! You're **always leaving** your clothes around. It's so untidy!
> HUSBAND: OK! OK! Calm down. Don't let's have an argument. You're **always complaining** these days.
> WIFE: Well, I'm not surprised – living with you!
> HUSBAND: Come on! You're **forever telling** me to relax. Why don't you try it?

Criticizing

This is a special use of the present continuous tense. We use the words **always, forever, continually** and **constantly** (they all mean 'all the time') when we want to suggest that something happens much more often than is normal. It is often used to criticize:

The secretary **is always** phoning her friends during office hours.
⟶ She phones her friends too often.

You're **forever losing** things.
⟶ You lose things too often.

NOTE	It is also possible to say:

The secretary always phones her friends during office hours.

This is a more neutral comment and not necessarily a criticism.

We put **always, forever, continually** and **constantly** before the main verb:

> 1   2
>
> Jenny is always arguing with her father.

11.2 Bird's eye box: Present continuous

> She's **writing (now).** ⟶ action happening now
>
> They're **always arguing.** ⟶ **always, forever, continually, constantly** for criticism

11.3 Present simple

do . . . do . . . ?

work

change, jog

train, play

do . . . find . . . ?

go

RONALD: What **do** you **do** in your spare time, Chris?

CHRIS: Well, every day I **work** till 5 o'clock. Then I usually **change** into my sports clothes and **jog** to the university. It's normally possible to use the sports hall even though I'm not a student. I **train** there quite regularly. I **play** squash whenever I can.

RONALD: How **do** you **find** time to do all this?

CHRIS: It's no problem. And I always **go** for a drink at the end of the evening.

───── **form** ─────

POSITIVE

infinitive + (other information)

| I | work | (hard enough). |
| You | | |

He		
She	stay s	(in the room).
It		

We		
You	live	(near here).
They		

NEGATIVE				⟶ SHORT FORM	
present simple of **do**	+ **not**	+ infinitive . . .			
I You	do	not	work . . .	I You	don't work . . .
He She It	does	not	stay . . .	He She It	doesn't stay . . .
We You They	do	not	live . . .	We You They	don't live . . .

QUESTION

present simple + infinitive . . . ?
of **do**

Do	I you	work . . . ?
Does	he she it	stay . . . ?
Do	we you they	live . . . ?

 When we speak we *often* use the negative short form:

I **don't go** out often.
He **doesn't drink** fruit juice.

| USE 1 |

Repeated action

When something happens regularly, sometimes, from time to time, or never, we show this by using the PRESENT SIMPLE.

> always   usually   often   normally   regularly
> sometimes   every day   never

These words are ADVERBS, or ADVERBIAL PHRASES, OF FREQUENCY (7.2–7.2.1) – they tell us how often an action takes place:

Paul **normally wears** very strong glasses.
I **usually change** into my sports clothes after work.
My sisters **never eat** bread or cakes.

Very often we do not need to use the adverbs:

Do you go to school?
How do you find all this?

In these cases we **understand** that the action of the verb is repeated – it is not necessary to put the adverb in.

USE 2

We also use the present simple tense when we want to make a general statement:

Iron **rusts** if you leave it in water.
Aerosol sprays **destroy** the ozone layer around the Earth.

11.4 Bird's eye box: Present simple

The car **often breaks down**.	⟶ repeated action
Onions make me cry.	⟶ general statement

11.5 Contrast between present continuous and present simple

 We use the present continuous tense to talk about something which is happening *now*. The present simple is a tense which we use when an action is *repeated* at more or less regular intervals:

Contrast

PRESENT CONTINUOUS *now*		PRESENT SIMPLE *repeated action*
I'm **drinking** my tea **now**.	⟷	**Normally I drink** coffee for breakfast.
Paul's **driving** to work **at the moment**.	⟷	He **often jogs** when he has time.
I'm **sitting** at my desk **for the time being**.	⟷	**Every afternoon I work** at my desk.
James **is playing** tennis **right now**.	⟷	He **always plays** tennis on Saturdays.

11.6 Bird's eye box: Present continuous/Present simple

> He's **speaking** to me ⟶ action happening now
> (**now**).
>
> He **speaks** to me every ⟶ repeated action
> day before I start work.

11.7 Stative verbs

do . . . see . . . ?

> JOHN: **Do** you **see** that man over at that table in the corner? What's he doing?
>
> IAN: He's having an argument with the waiter. I think he's complaining about his soup.
>
> JOHN: You're right. He's shouting at the waiter. He's saying that it **tastes** terrible. Can you hear what he's saying now?
>
> IAN: Yes. He's telling the waiter that there's a fly in his soup. He **doesn't see** why he should pay for it!

tastes

doesn't see

1 Some verbs are usually used only in the simple tenses. They refer to states rather than actions. They are rarely used in the continuous form:

verbs of the senses

hear	feel	see	smell	taste

I **hear** the sound of gun-fire. The cake **smells** good.

This pullover **feels** really soft. The wine **tastes** very sweet.

We only use these verbs in the continuous form to emphasize that a state is temporary or unusual:

I bumped my head and now I'**m seeing** stars!

You'**re smelling** very nice! What's the name of your perfume?

I'**m feeling** wonderful today.

2 The following verbs are also usually used in the simple form only:

verbs of emotion

dislike	hate	like	love	want	wish

verbs of the mind

believe	doubt	fear	feel	know	mean	mind
prefer	remember	see	suppose	understand		

I **believe** you are the man I'm looking for.

She **knows** now what she has done wrong.

Paul **doesn't mind** if you use his car.

Do you **remember** me now?

I **see** the point.
⟶ I understand the point.

He **feels** that he is right.
⟶ He is of the opinion that he is right.

 3 The following verbs are also not usually used in the continuous form:

appear	belong to	concern	depend on	include
involve	need	owe	own	possess	resemble	seem

He **appears** to be climbing through the window.

She **doesn't possess** a thing in the world.

 4 Some of these verbs can be used in the continuous form when they show that a process is taking place gradually or that a situation is temporary:

I'm on holiday in Blackpool and I**'m loving** every minute.

I**'m** slowly **remembering** all the details of the accident.

Look, a rabbit **is appearing** from the magician's hat.

Notice the difference in meaning between:

He **feels** he is right.
⟶ It is his opinion that he is right.

He **feels** fine now.
⟶ His state of health is good.

 5 be and have

be is not used in the continuous form when it describes a state or situation:

He **is** at home now.

She **was** at the party yesterday.

131

But we can use the continuous form to show that a certain kind of behaviour is temporary or unusual:

They**'re being** very silly.
He**'s being** very noisy.
What is the matter? You**'re being** very quiet!

have is not used in the continuous form when it means 'possess' or 'own':

I **have** a Renault 5 motor car.

have is used in the continuous form when it does not mean 'possess' (see OTHER MEANINGS OF **have**, 9.6.2):

They**'re having** an argument.
She**'s having** a wash.
Jim and Jean **are having** tea.

11.8 Bird's eye box: Stative verbs

hear feel see smell taste	⟶	sense verbs
believe doubt fear know mean etc.	⟶	mind verbs
dislike like want love etc.	⟶	emotion verbs

11.9 Imperative

	PASSENGER: Could you tell me where I have to give in my luggage, please?
take, put	CLERK: **Take** it to check-in number 9, please. **Put** it on
wait	the scales and **wait** for the clerk. She'll weigh it for
don't forget	you. And **don't forget** to keep all your valuables with
don't leave	you. **Don't leave** them in your luggage.
	PASSENGER: What do I have to do after that?
take	CLERK: You'll be given a boarding card. **Take** it with
go	you and **go** to gate number 7.
let's hurry	PASSENGER: (*to friend*) Come on, David. **Let's hurry** a
bring	bit. We're late. **Bring** the second suitcase.

—————————— **form** ——————————

(**don't**)	+ infinitive	+	(other information)
	| Pull	|	(harder).
	| Stop	|	(shouting).
Don't	| talk	|	(with your mouth full).
Don't	| drink and drive.		

USE

Orders/invitations/instructions

We use the IMPERATIVE form when we want to order or command somebody to do something:

Close the door, please.   **Don't sit** there.

to invite somebody:

Come round for a glass of wine.

to give instructions (e.g. on a machine):

Press the red button and **wait**.

 1 do

We put **do** in front of the main verb to give extra emphasis:

Do come and visit me.   ⟶ Please come, I really want you to.
Do be more careful.   ⟶ Please try to be more careful.

We also use the long form of the negative, **do not**, for emphasis. The stress falls on **not**:

Do **not** come home late again.
⟶ You must never again come home late.

 2 let's

A very polite form of command, which is more of a suggestion, can be made with **let's** (**let us**). The speaker intends taking part in the action, too:

Let's try to run in a marathon.
⟶ Why don't we try running in a marathon?

Let's start this again.
⟶ I think it would be a good idea if we started this again.

Let's go! ⟶ We must go./I think we should go.

11.10 Bird's eye box: Imperative

Speak louder (please). ⎱ (Please) **don't argue.** ⎰	⟶ order/command (more polite with **please**
Join us for drinks.	⟶ invitation
Stir the mixture with a spoon.	⟶ instruction
Do **hurry.** ⎱ **Do** *not* **fidget.** ⎰	⟶ **do (not)** for emphasis
Let's have a holiday.	⟶ suggestion

11.11 Past simple (simple past) (point of time)

	New Year's Eve in Germany
was, spent	Last week it **was** New Year's Eve and we **spent** this
was	holiday in West Berlin. It **was** a new experience for us.
bought	First of all, everybody **bought** a lot of fireworks. Then on
gathered	the evening of 31st December people **gathered** in groups
ate	of friends and **ate** New Year's dinner or buffet meals. At
stopped	12 o'clock, midnight, the meals and dancing **stopped**.
drank, wished	Then everybody **drank** together and **wished** each other
	'Happy New Year'. A moment later thousands of
went	fireworks **went** off in the sky above the city. At about 2
started	o'clock in the morning people **started** eating cakes. They
drank, didn't want	also **drank** strong coffee. Probably they **didn't want** to fall
	asleep.

─────────── **form** ───────────

POSITIVE

infinitive + **ed/d** + (other information)

I			
You			
He			
She	appear___ed	(round the corner).
It	move___d	(slowly).
We			
You			
They			

- - - - - - - - - - - - - - - - - - - -

NEGATIVE   → SHORT FORM

past simple
of **do** + **not** + infinitive...

I				I	
You				You	
He				He	
She	did	not	appear...	She	didn't appear...
It				It	
We				We	
You				You	
They				They	

QUESTION

past simple + infinitive . . . ?
of **do**

Did | I / you / he / she / it / we / you / they | appear . . . ?

1 Irregular verbs

Irregular verbs do not take **ed** or **d**. Their form changes in other ways:

go ⟶ I **went**   **see** ⟶ he **saw**
run ⟶ she **ran**   **ring** ⟶ the phone **rang**

The negative and question forms of irregular verbs are made in the same way as with regular verbs, using the infinitive:

They **didn't go** to the cinema.
Did you **see** the football match?

| USE |

Finished action at a known time

When we want to say that a completed action took place at a definite time in the past we use the PAST SIMPLE (SIMPLE PAST). Often there is an ADVERBIAL PHRASE (7.1) in the sentence which tells us exactly when the action took place:

```
     action          time of action
I saw the moon     last night.
```

```
          action                      time of action
I didn't know the answer     last week (but I do now).
```

```
       action                 time of action
She was on television     two hours ago.
```

We use expressions like the following to give definite time information:

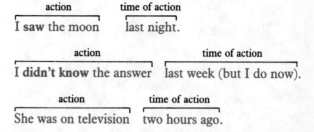

last week   yesterday   last year   two days ago
when I was a boy   when I was at school   from . . . to

PAST TIME | NOW

I **had** an accident in my car **last week**.

2   The verb **be** is special because:

1   The first and third persons singular have the form **was** while the other persons have the form **were** (9.2.2):

(singular)
I was very nervous about it.
You were the last person I
  expected to see.
He was later than usual.
She was here yesterday.
It was the last opportunity.

(plural)
We were at home last night.
You were both marvellous!
They were here just a moment
  ago.

2   We make negative sentences with **not**:

She **was not** (**wasn't**) here.   They **were not** (**weren't**) here.

3   We change the word order when we make a question:

```
 1   2    3            2    1   3
She was here.  ——→  Was she here?
```

```
 1    2     3            2    1   3
They were late.  ——→  Were they late?
```

11.11.1   Past simple (period of time)

	DAVID: Were you in the army when you were younger, John?
served wore	JOHN: I was, actually, just for a couple of years. I **served** from 1952 to 1954. I **wore** a uniform for two years. But you didn't join, did you?
lived worked had	DAVID: No. At that time I **lived** in Africa. In fact I **worked** for an English company in Nigeria from 1952 until 1959. I **had** the job for seven years. It was an interesting time.
lived	JOHN: So you **lived** in Africa for seven years. Why did you come back to Europe?

USE

Finished action during a known time

The past simple can be used when an action began in the past, continued for a definite period of time, and then finished:

I **lived** in Africa **from** 1952 **to** 1959.
I **lived** in Africa **for** seven years.

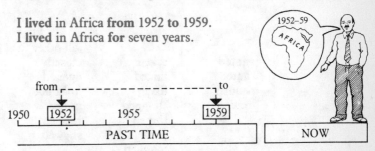

11.12 Bird's eye box: Past simple

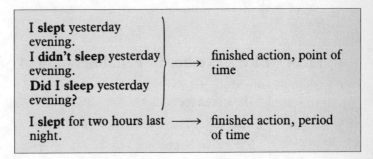

I **slept** yesterday evening. I **didn't sleep** yesterday evening. **Did I sleep** yesterday evening?	⟶ finished action, point of time
I **slept** for two hours last night.	⟶ finished action, period of time

11.13 Pronunciation of past simple (regular verbs)

showed
decided

MO: Come on. I **showed** you what's on at the cinema and we **decided** to go to *Odyssey 2000*. Don't you remember?

tried, intended
wanted
finished

MARC: I **tried** to explain that I **intended** to work this evening. I **wanted** to finish a chapter of my book.
MO: Haven't you **finished** that book yet?

 There are three ways of pronouncing the past simple endings of verbs:

WE WRITE	WE SAY	WE WRITE	WE SAY	WE WRITE	WE SAY
painted	⟶ paintid	asked	⟶ askt	closed	⟶ closd
wanted	⟶ wantid	mixed	⟶ mixt	opened	⟶ opend
mended	⟶ mendid	shopped	⟶ shopt		

It is necessary to consider the last letters of the infinitive and the sound that they make:

/ɪd/	/t/	/d/
		(all other final letters)
painted	asked	closed
wanted	mixed	opened
mended	fixed	imagined
decided	shopped	pulled
	tipped	rubbed
	pushed	showed
	touched	
	passed	
	laughed	
	watched	

11.14 Bird's eye box: Pronunciation of past simple

He wait**ed** for me.	⟶ /ɪd/
They pass**ed** us without waving.	⟶ /t/
She yell**ed** but no one heard.	⟶ /d/

11.15 Past continuous (interrupted by past simple)

The robber who fell asleep on a bank raid

was taking
was . . . lying
was holding

was holding

A robber broke into a bank and then fell asleep while he **was taking** the money out of the safe. When the police arrived at the bank, the robber **was** already **lying** on the floor. When the police woke him he **was holding** £2.64 in his hand. His solicitor explained that the man had in fact quite a lot of money in his account. 'Why did he try to rob the bank, then?' An Inspector explained, 'When we arrested him he **was holding** a bottle of whisky.'

Adapted from the *Daily Telegraph*, 12 January 1984.

---- **form** ----

POSITIVE

past simple of **be**	+	present participle (infinitive + **ing**)	+	(other information)

I	was	read_____ing	(a book).
You	were	laugh_____ing	(heartily).

He			
She	was	stand_____ing	(outside).
It			

We			
You	were	knock_____ing	(on the door).
They			

NEGATIVE   ⟶   SHORT FORM

past simple + **not** + present
of **be**   participle . . .

I	was	not	reading . . .	I wasn't reading . . .
You	were	not	laughing . . .	You weren't laughing . . .

He				He	
She	was	not	standing . . .	She	wasn't standing . . .
It				It	

We				We	
You	were	not	knocking . . .	You	weren't knocking . . .
They				They	

QUESTION

past simple + present participle . . . ?
of **be**

Was	I	reading . . . ?
Were	you	laughing . . . ?

	he	
Was	she	standing . . . ?
	it	

	we	
Were	you	trying . . . ?
	they	

USE

One past action interrupted by another

We use the PAST CONTINUOUS to describe a past action which is interrupted by another past action. This second action is described by the PAST SIMPLE (11.11):

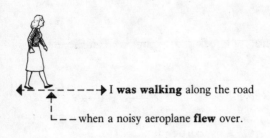

←- - - - - →I **was walking** along the road

└ - - when a noisy aeroplane **flew** over.

PAST TIME	NOW

The interrupted action (in the past continuous) lasted longer than the action which interrupted it (in the past simple):

longer action   shorter action

I **was watching** television when the phone rang.

11.15.1 Past continuous (followed by past continuous)

USE

Two past actions continuing together

Sometimes two past actions continued for some time together. In such cases we use the past continuous tense for *both* actions:

I **was writing** a business letter while she **was sleeping** in front of the television.

She **was lying** on a beach in Greece while I **was working** in an office in London.

Were you **reading** the paper while I **was bringing** the shopping from the car?

When we use the past continuous tense in the two ways described here and in 11.15, we often use the following linking words to connect the two actions concerned.

while   just as   at the same time as   when

first action (continuous)   second action (simple)

What **were** you **doing when** the murder **took place?**

first action (continuous)   second action (continuous)

I **was waiting** here **while** you **were playing** football.

11.15.2 Past continuous (more emphatic than past simple)

USE

Past action over a period of time

The past continuous is used to describe an action in the past which continued over a length of time. The PAST SIMPLE (11.11.1) can be used in a similar way but the past continuous places greater emphasis on the length of time:

I **worked** all yesterday evening. (neutral statement)

I **was working** all yesterday evening! (emphasis on the fact that it was a very long time to be working)

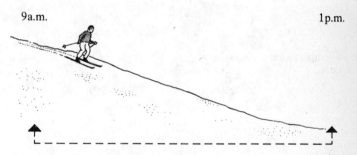

9a.m.   1p.m.

I **was skiing** all yesterday morning.
I **was skiing** for four hours.

11.16 Bird's eye box: Past continuous

I **was working** when she came in.	→ two past actions, one interrupted by the other
I **was working** while she **was swimming**.	→ two past actions continuing together
I **was playing** tennis for six hours yesterday!	→ action continuing in past (emphatic)

141

11.17 Present perfect (complete)

has told, 've given	FATHER: Your mother **has told** me that you**'ve given** up your job. You don't want to work any more. What are your plans?
've decided	JOHN: Yes – that's right. I**'ve decided** to drive a camping bus across Europe and the Middle East to India. It's
've . . . wanted	something I**'ve** always **wanted** to do. I**'ve saved**
've saved	enough money and I'm going to do it.
've talked	FATHER: I**'ve talked** to your mother and she's very unhappy about what you're doing. Please think again.
've thought	JOHN: I**'ve thought** about it very carefully and it's my decision.

---
form

POSITIVE   ⟶ SHORT FORM

present simple + past   participle   + (other
  of **have**   (infinitive + **ed/d**)   information)

I		have	finish	ed	(writing).	I've		finished...
You			decide	d	(to leave).	You've		decided...
He			collect	ed	(the rubbish).	He's		collected...
She		has	complete	d	(the washing).	She's		completed...
It						It's		completed...
We			fill	ed	(the bag).	We've		filled...
You		have	move	d	(the car).	You've		moved...
They			move	d		They've		moved...

NEGATIVE   ⟶ SHORT FORM (1)   SHORT FORM (2)

present simple + **not** + past
  of **have**   participle...

I		have	not	finished...	I		haven't	I've		not
You					You		finished...	You've		finished...
He					He		hasn't	He's		not
She		has	not	collected...	She		collected...	She's		collected...
It					It			It's		
We					We		haven't	We've		not
You		have	not	filled...	You		filled...	You've		filled...
They					They			They've		

QUESTION

present simple + past participle...?
  of **have**

| Have | I | finished... ? |
| | you | |

Has	he	
	she	collected... ?
	it	

Have	we	
	you	filled... ?
	they	

If the main verb is regular, the PAST PARTICIPLE
16.3–16.5 is formed by adding **ed** or **d** to the infinitive,
exactly like the PAST SIMPLE (11.11). Irregular verbs have
irregular past participles, sometimes the same as, sometimes
different from, their past simple form:

INFINITIVE	PAST SIMPLE	PAST PARTICIPLE
walk	walked	walked
move	moved	moved
make	made	made
see	saw	seen

See Appendix.

Finished action at an unknown time

We use the PRESENT PERFECT to describe an action which
finished at some time in the past but we don't know exactly
when. (The time is **not** important.)

I've often **visited** Japan.
⟶ But we don't know exactly when each visit happened.

She's **been** here.
⟶ No time information but the action is finished.

11.17.1 Contrast between present perfect and past simple

We can make a contrast with the PAST SIMPLE (11.11–11.14).
Both tenses describe an action which finished in the past, but
we use the past simple when we know *when* the action
finished. Consequently, with the past simple we often use
ADVERBS or ADVERBIAL PHRASES OF DEFINITE TIME (7.1)
like **yesterday, last year**, etc.

Contrast	
PRESENT PERFECT	PAST SIMPLE
I've **heard** something about the war.	I **heard** something about the war on the news **yesterday evening**.
She's **passed** the exam.	She **passed** the exam **in April**.
(no time information)	(time information about when the action finished)

DANGER | The following adverbs/adverbial phrases can be used with either tense:

> today   this year   this week   this morning
> this evening   lately   recently

PRESENT PERFECT	PAST SIMPLE
I've **seen** a film about motor racing this morning.	I **saw** a film about motor racing this morning.
⟶ It is still morning, the morning is the present.	⟶ It is no longer morning. Perhaps it is afternoon and the action finished at a definite time in the past.

 We often use the present perfect with the adverbs **already** and **just** when the action has finished:

She's **just** found a new job.
They've **already** polluted half the world.

11.17.2 Present perfect (incomplete) (for and since)

for . . .'ve had

have . . . had
since

've played . . .
for

> DOCTOR: What is the problem then, Mr Jones?
> MR JONES: Well, *for* the last 3 days I've **had** a pain at the bottom of my back. It begins here and goes down into my leg.
> DOCTOR: How long **have** you **had** it in your leg?
> MR JONES: *Since* last Friday, I think.
> DOCTOR: Have you lifted anything very heavy or taken any unusual exercise?
> MR JONES: I don't think so. I've **played** tennis every week *for* years. I've never had any problems before.

USE | ### Unfinished action

We use the present perfect to describe an action which began in the past and continues in the present:

I've **learnt** Japanese for two years.

2 years ago

PAST TIME	NOW

I began to learn Japanese and I'm still learning **now**.

Paul **has played** in a band since Easter.
⟶ He still plays in the band.
This building **has been** here for three hundred years.
I**'ve taught** languages for ten years.
How long **have** you **been** in England?
⟶ You came to England in the past but you are still here.

for and since

We often use the words **for** and **since** with the present perfect
(including the PRESENT PERFECT CONTINUOUS (11.19)):

for is followed by a length of time (e.g. **a year, ten days**).
since is followed by a point of time (e.g. **last week, six
o'clock, yesterday**).

They**'ve discussed** this **for** years. ⟶ period of time
Have you **seen** her **since** the accident? ⟶ point of time

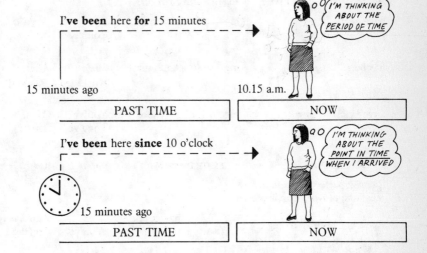

11.18 Bird's eye box: Present perfect

He**'s** often **eaten** in that restaurant.	⟶	finished action, unspecified time
I**'ve just given up** my job.	⟶	finished action with **just/already**
The new manager **has been** here **for** six weeks.	⟶	unfinished action with **for**
The new manager **has been** here **since** July.	⟶	unfinished action with **since**

11.19 Present perfect continuous (incomplete)

've been reading

've been watching

've been reading

> JUDITH: You**'ve been reading** that newspaper for the last hour. I hate it when you read at breakfast.
>
> PETER: Yes, and you**'ve been watching** me the whole time. And you know it's a very important time of the day for me. I need to relax before I begin the day's work.
>
> JUDITH: OK, but think of me. I**'ve been reading** the back of your morning newspaper for ten years now and I'd like someone to talk to!

---

form

POSITIVE ⟶ **SHORT FORM**

present perfect + of **be**	present participle (infinitive + **ing**)	+ (other information)		
I You	have been	try____ing	(since yesterday).	I've You've	been trying...
He She It	has been	work____ing	(for ten hours).	He's She's It's	been working...
We You They	have been	sing____ing	(all afternoon).	We've You've They've	been singing...

NEGATIVE ⟶ **SHORT FORM (1)**   **SHORT FORM (2)**

present perfect + negative of **be**	present participle ...				
I You	have not been	trying...	I You	haven't been trying...	I've You've	not been trying...
He She It	has not been	working...	He She It	hasn't been working...	He's She's It's	not been working...
We You They	have not been	singing...	We You They	haven't been singing...	We've You've They've	not been singing...

QUESTION				
present perfect question of **be**			+ present participle... ?	
Have	I you	been	trying... ?	
Has	he she it	been	working... ?	
Have	we you they	been	singing... ?	

USE

Unfinished action

In the text opposite and above the examples are of action that began in the past and is still going on.

He began to read the newspaper (and he's still reading it).

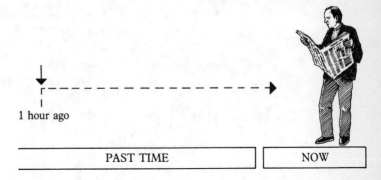

1 hour ago

PAST TIME	NOW

He's **been reading** the newspaper for an hour.

She's **been studying** for ten years.

Have they **been swimming** since early this morning?

When we want to describe an action which began some time in the past and we want to make clear that this action is continuing at the present moment (when the speaker is speaking), we use the PRESENT PERFECT CONTINUOUS:

JENNY: **I've been looking** for you. I didn't know you were in the living room. How long have you been watching television?

PAUL: **I've been sitting** here for more than an hour.

See also the PRESENT PERFECT (INCOMPLETE) (11.17.2).

11.19.1 Present perfect continuous (result)

have...been
doing?
'''ve been playing
'''ve been throwing

'''ve been playing

> MOTHER: What on earth **have** you **been doing?** You're covered in ink. Your clothes are ruined.
> LITTLE BOY: We**'ve been playing** Cowboys and Indians.
> MOTHER: You mean you**'ve been throwing** ink around. What's ink got to do with cowboys?
> LITTLE BOY: Well, I**'ve been playing** with a water pistol and my ammunition was ink.

USE

Recently finished action

When we want to say that an action began in the past and continued until a few moments ago, and we can *see* the result of the action, we use the present perfect continuous. In the text above, the little boy is no longer playing Cowboys and Indians but his mother can see the result of this action – that he is covered in ink.

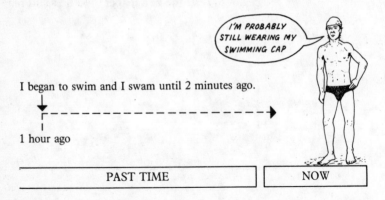

I began to swim and I swam until 2 minutes ago.

1 hour ago

| PAST TIME | NOW |

I'm probably still wearing my swimming cap

I've been swimming.

11.20 Bird's eye box: Present perfect continuous

I've **been reading for** ten minutes.	⟶ unfinished action with **for**
He's **been shouting since** nine o'clock.	⟶ unfinished action with **since**
I've **been drinking** tea.	⟶ recently finished action

11.21 Contrast between present perfect continuous and present perfect

> The two teams | **have been playing** | for thirty-five
> | **have played** | minutes.
>
> Neither has scored a goal. I hope Norwich can win
> this game because I've wanted them to get the
> championship since the first time I saw them play. I've
> belonged to the official fan club for more than six years
> and I've always known they would manage it one day.
>
> Now the match is finished. The final score is 0:0 and
>
> I've | **been wasting** | my time watching this terrible
> | **wasted** |
>
> game for an hour and a half.

The present perfect continuous and present perfect tenses have
almost the same meaning only when we use them with **for** and
since. In the text above we see that the two football teams **have
played** or **have been playing** for thirty-five minutes. The
meaning is almost the same. (They began playing in the past
and they are still playing.)

The present perfect continuous is used more often when the
action is likely to continue into the future.

They've **been arguing** since breakfast (and are likely to
continue).

They've **argued** since breakfast (and I hope that they can now
stop).

Very often the difference between the two tenses with **for** and
since is very slight and a question of style. Some verbs,
however, are almost never used in the continuous (see STATIVE
VERBS, 11.7).

11.22   Past perfect

had continued

had heard

had arrived

had cost

> The great petrol pump swindle **had continued** for two years before the government finally did something about it. Many car drivers **had heard** that it was possible to buy a special machine which could change the figures on the petrol pumps. After the driver **had arrived** in the petrol station he simply switched on his machine. The machine controlled the figures on the self-service pumps and the drivers paid for less petrol than they really got.
> This swindle **had cost** the petrol companies millions of pounds before they realized.
>
> Adapted from the *Daily Express*, 29 October 1983.

--- form ---

POSITIVE ⟶ SHORT FORM

past simple + past participle + (other information)
  of **have** (infinitive + ed/d)

I						I'd	
You						You'd	
He						He'd	
She	had	accept	ed	(the invitation)		She'd	accepted . . .
It		announce	d	(the winner).		It'd	announced . . .
We						We'd	
You						You'd	
They						They'd	

- -

NEGATIVE ⟶ SHORT FORM (1)   SHORT FORM (2)

past simple + **not** + past
  of **have**   participle . . .

I				I		I'd	
You				You		You'd	
He				He		He'd	
She	had	not	accepted . . .	She	hadn't	She'd	not
It				It	accepted. . .	It'd	accepted . . .
We				We		We'd	
You				You		You'd	
They				They		They'd	

- -

QUESTION

past simple of **have** + past participle . . . ?

	I	
	you	
	he	
Had	she	accepted . . . ?
	it	
	we	
	you	
	they	

USE	**Two past actions – one finished before the other began**

When we want to talk about two actions which happened in the past and one of the these finished earlier than the other we use the PAST PERFECT:

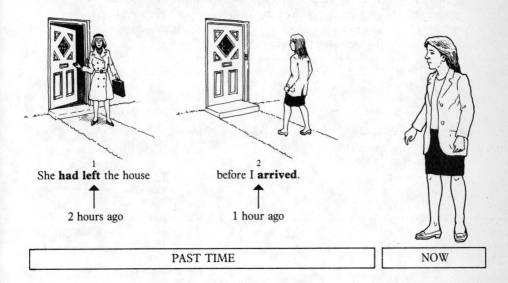

She **had left** the house
2 hours ago

before I **arrived**.
1 hour ago

PAST TIME	NOW

The earlier action is in the past perfect, the later action in the PAST SIMPLE (11.11).

 We often use the past perfect with these TIME LINKING WORDS (23.2):

after   before   as soon as   when

first action   second action

As soon as he'd **seen** the policeman, he **began** to get nervous.

first action   second action

Before she'd **signed** the document, the police **rushed** through the door.

11.23 Bird's eye box: Past perfect

I'd **known** the answer before she told me.	⟶	first of two past actions

11.24   Past perfect continuous

had been working
had been trying
hadn't been
practising

When the new student arrived, he said that he **had been working** in a bank for five years. He **had been trying** to learn English at an evening class but **hadn't been practising** spoken English very much. He admitted that after every class he used to go for a drink and speak French with his classmates!

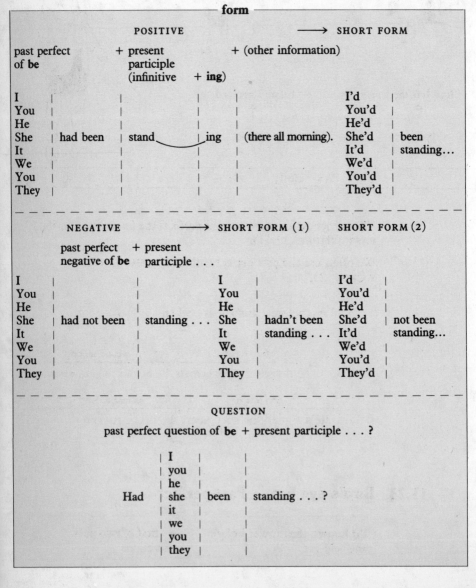

────── **form** ──────

POSITIVE   ⟶ SHORT FORM

past perfect   + present   + (other information)
of **be**   participle
                 (infinitive   + **ing**)

I					I'd	
You					You'd	
He					He'd	
She	had been	stand	ing	(there all morning).	She'd	been
It					It'd	standing...
We					We'd	
You					You'd	
They					They'd	

NEGATIVE   ⟶ SHORT FORM (1)   SHORT FORM (2)

past perfect   + present
negative of **be**   participle . . .

I			I		I'd	
You			You		You'd	
He			He		He'd	
She	had not been	standing . . .	She	hadn't been	She'd	not been
It			It	standing . . .	It'd	standing...
We			We		We'd	
You			You		You'd	
They			They		They'd	

QUESTION

past perfect question of **be** + present participle . . . ?

	I		
	you		
	he		
Had	she	been	standing . . . ?
	it		
	we		
	you		
	they		

USE	**Two past actions – one continued until the second began**

The PAST PERFECT CONTINUOUS is used to show that one past action took place over a period of time before another past action began.

In many situations we can use the PAST PERFECT (11.22–11.23) or the PAST PERFECT CONTINUOUS for the action which happened first.

He'd **played** tennis for an hour before his wife telephoned.
or
He'd **been playing** tennis for an hour before she arrived.

We use the past perfect continuous when we want to emphasize that the earlier action continued until the later action began.

In the pictures below the detective asks:
How long **had** you **been standing** in front of the bank when you heard the alarm bell?

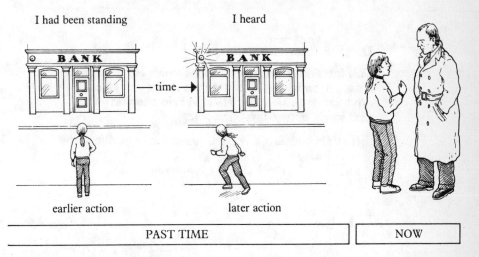

I had been standing   I heard

← time →

earlier action   later action

PAST TIME   NOW

I **had been standing** there for about five minutes when I **heard** the alarm bell.

11.25 Bird's eye box: Past perfect continuous

He'd **been hoping** to pass the exam before he got the result.	⟶	first of two past actions, continuing until the second began.

11.26 Present continuous for the future

is leaving

is expecting

are discussing

> The Prime Minister **is leaving** for Brussels tomorrow to attend an EEC conference. The Minister of Defence will accompany her. The talks will probably last two days. The Prime Minister herself **is expecting** a difficult debate, particularly on the second day when they **are discussing** the question of defence strategy.

——— **form** ———

present continuous	+ future adverb/adverbial phrase of time
I'm seeing the dentist	tomorrow afternoon.
He's phoning me again	this time next week.
The council meeting **is taking** place	tomorrow at ten.
We're leaving on the Brussels train	at nine o'clock.

USE

Definite future arrangements

This form describes future actions which are clearly and definitely arranged. With it we use future ADVERBS/ ADVERBIAL PHRASES OF TIME (7.1) like **tomorrow, next week, in two days' time**, etc.

JOHN: Do you have any plans to see the latest film at the Roxy?

JEAN: Yes, I have. **I'm going tomorrow.**

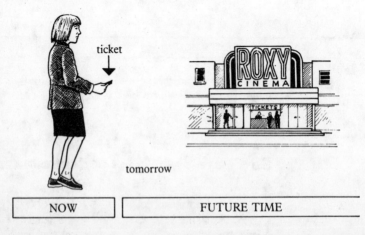

ticket

tomorrow

NOW	FUTURE TIME

See 11.1 for the FORM of the PRESENT CONTINUOUS.

11.27 will (future)

'll clean

'll wash
'll finish
'll have

> JANE: I'll **clean** the car later on this afternoon. Do you
> want to help me?
> DAVID: Well, I don't have a lot of time at the moment,
> but I'll **wash** the windows for you if you want.
> JANE: Good. If we work together we'll **finish** it by 3
> o'clock. That means I'll **have** time to change for the
> party.
> DAVID: Party? What party? Do you mean that I have to
> help you so that you can go to a party without me?
> What a cheek!

---
form

POSITIVE   ⟶   SHORT FORM

will + infinitive + (other information)

I				I'll	
You				You'll	
He				He'll	
She	will	arrive	(in the morning).	She'll	arrive . . .
It				It'll	
We				We'll	
You				You'll	
They				They'll	

NEGATIVE   ⟶   SHORT FORM (1)   SHORT FORM (2)

will + **not** + infinitive . . .

I				I		I'll	
You				You		You'll	
He				He		He'll	
She	will	not	arrive . . .	She	won't	She'll	not
It				It	arrive . . .	It'll	arrive . . .
We				We		We'll	
You				You		You'll	
They				They		They'll	

QUESTION

will   + infinitive . . . ?

	I	
	you	
	he	
Will	she	arrive . . . ?
	it	
	we	
	you	
	they	

We can also use **shall** with the same meaning as **will** with **I** and **we** when talking about the future.

I **shall** speak. *or* I'**ll** speak. *or* I **will** speak.

We **shall** arrive. *or* We'**ll** arrive. *or* We **will** arrive.

USE 1

Willingness to do something in the future

will is used when we want to say that we are willing to do something in the future. It is often used in this sense for offers of help:

I'**ll give** you a lift to the party.
I'**ll wash** the windows for you.

We can offer other people's services, too:

My husband **will help** you with your garden.

See also **will** as a MODAL VERB (10.2).

USE 2

Future possibilities

The **will** future is used to describe future speculations and possibilities. We use it for future events about which we feel uncertain. It is often found with verbs such as **think, feel, hope, promise, imagine**, etc.

He **hopes** he'**ll wake up** in time for the bus.
I **promise** I **won't forget** you.

The **will** future is therefore often found in CONDITIONAL SENTENCES (19.1):

If the waiter doesn't hurry with the food, we'**ll go** somewhere else.

USE 3

Spontaneous decisions

The **will** future is often used to describe instant decisions which had no previous plan (this is the opposite of the **going to** FUTURE (11.28)):

I don't know where to go this evening. Oh! I'**ll ring** Jim and invite him round.
———→ a sudden decision, unplanned

What should we eat this evening? I know, I'**ll cook** spaghetti!

USE 4

Definite future actions

will can be used to talk about definite future actions at a mentioned time. We often use it to confirm appointments:

I'll see you **at eight tomorrow**.   'Bye! **I'll see** you **later**.

In more formal (and often assertive) English, **will** can be used to speak about definite future plans:

PRIME MINISTER: The government **will** lower all taxes, and I **will** ensure that every family in this country **will** benefit.

In everyday English we do not normally announce future arrangements about ourselves with **will**. The PRESENT CONTINUOUS (11.1) sounds more natural:

I will leave England in June. ⟶ formal
I'm leaving England in June. ⟶ more natural

However, in announcements of timetables, schedules and other future programmes (11.33), **will** can be used:

Flight 214 **will** be departing in twenty minutes.

11.28 going to (future)

are ... going
to ... ?

TEACHER: Well, Marc. What **are** you **going to** do when you go back to Switzerland?
MARC: Left, right; left, right; left, right!
TEACHER: Pardon?

'm going to

MARC: I'm **going to** join the army – I have to do my military service!
TEACHER: Oh. I understand now. What about you, Michael?

'm going to
'm going to

MICHAEL: First **I'm going to** have a holiday and then **I'm going to** look for a new job.

form

POSITIVE				SHORT FORM	
present simple + **going to** + infinitive + (other material)					
of **be**					
I	am	going to	ask	(the teacher).	I'm	going to ask...
You	are	going to	buy	(the vegetables).	You're	going to buy...
He					He's	
She	is	going to	remain	(there).	She's	going to remain...
It					It's	
We					We're	
You	are	going to	visit	(the castle).	You're	going to visit...
They					They're	

TENSES OF THE VERB (ACTIVE)

NEGATIVE				⟶	SHORT FORM (1)		SHORT FORM (2)	
present simple + not + going to + infinitive . . . of **be**								
I	am	not	going to	ask...	—		I'm	not going to ask...
You	are	not	going to	buy...	You	aren't going to buy...	You're	not going to buy...
He She It	is	not	going to	remain...	He She It	isn't going to remain...	He's She's It's	not going to remain...
We You They	are	not	going to	visit...	We You They	aren't going to visit...	We're You're They're	not going to visit...

QUESTION

present simple + going to + infinitive . . . ? of **be**

Am	I	going to	ask . . . ?
Are	you	going to	buy . . . ?
Is	he she it	going to	remain . . . ?
Are	we you they	going to	visit . . . ?

USE

Future intentions/plans

The **going to** future shows that we have a clear plan in our mind. We intend to do something in the future:

I'm going to have a party next weekend.
⟶ I have a plan to have a party.

He's going to buy a second-hand car.
⟶ He intends to buy a second-hand car.

Notice the difference in meaning between:

PRESENT CONTINUOUS

I'm buying a new car on Saturday.
⟶ It is arranged, already organized.

going to FUTURE

I'm going to buy a new car on Saturday.
⟶ I intend to buy one, but I have no particular car in mind.

158

11.29 Future continuous

> GABY: I've arranged a holiday abroad this year. I'm going to Greece for six weeks. I fly there on June 5th.
>
> JAMES: June 5th? That's the day I begin my new job. Just think, as you fly out of England **I'll be putting on** my new suit and **trying** to look like a real banker!
>
> GABY: Well, you'll earn plenty of money. But just think. When you're sitting behind your desk **I'll be lying** on a beach in twenty-seven degrees of sun.
>
> JAMES: Well, at least send me a postcard.

'll be putting
on . . . trying

'll be lying

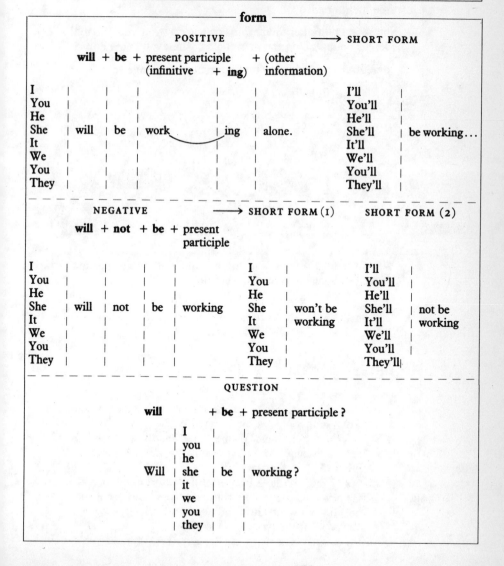

───── **form** ─────

POSITIVE ⟶ **SHORT FORM**

will + **be** + present participle + (other
(infinitive + **ing**) information)

I	will	be	work~ing	alone.	I'll	be working...
You					You'll	
He					He'll	
She					She'll	
It					It'll	
We					We'll	
You					You'll	
They					They'll	

NEGATIVE ⟶ **SHORT FORM (1)** **SHORT FORM (2)**

will + **not** + **be** + present
participle

I	will	not	be	working	I	won't be working	I'll	not be working
You					You		You'll	
He					He		He'll	
She					She		She'll	
It					It		It'll	
We					We		We'll	
You					You		You'll	
They					They		They'll	

QUESTION

will + **be** + present participle ?

Will	I	be	working ?
	you		
	he		
	she		
	it		
	we		
	you		
	they		

USE

A continuous action at a fixed time in the future

The FUTURE CONTINUOUS describes a continuous action at a fixed time in the future. The future time can be precise, or indicated by an ADVERBIAL CLAUSE of time (23.2.1) or an ADVERBIAL PHRASE (7.1).

I'll be sitting in the hairdresser's at two o'clock on Saturday. (precise time)
I'll be waiting at the station when your train arrives. (adverbial clause of time in present simple)
What will you be doing this time next week? (adverbial phrase)

Usually the continuous action is completed after the point in time mentioned:

She'll be taking her final exams on the day you get married.
They'll be installing the new cooker when you come home.

Sometimes the shorter action interrupts the longer one.

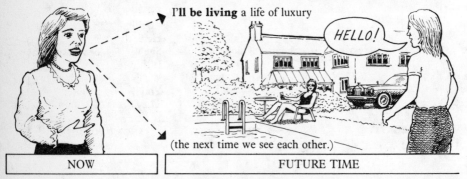

I'll be living a life of luxury

HELLO!

(the next time we see each other.)

NOW	FUTURE TIME

When the fixed time is a length of time (not a point of time), the action takes place within that time:

	on Saturday.
I'll be working	tomorrow.
	(all) next week.

11.30 Future perfect

'll have
finished ... by
'll have written ... by
will have paid

CELIA: When can we meet for a meal and a glass of wine? When will you have some free time?
SUE: What about next Wednesday? That'll give me three days to finish writing my essay. I'm sure I'll have finished it by then.
CELIA: Fine, I'll have written my next essay by then too – and what's more my father will have paid my next month's allowance into the bank and I'll actually be able to afford a pizza!

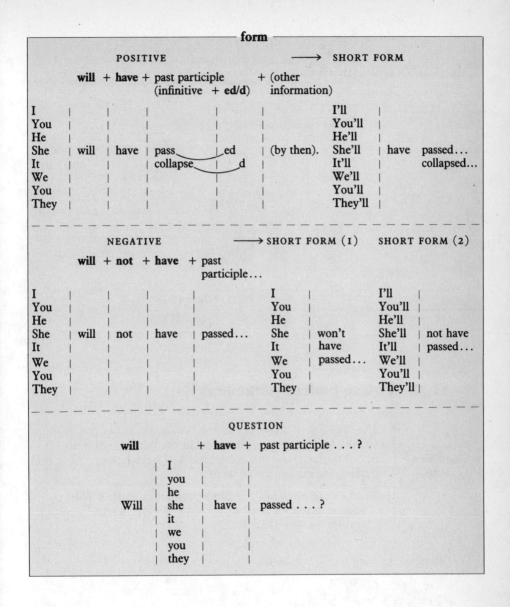

―――― **form** ――――

POSITIVE ⟶ SHORT FORM

will + have + past participle + (other
(infinitive + ed/d) information)

I						I'll	
You						You'll	
He						He'll	
She	will	have	pass___ed		(by then).	She'll	have passed...
It			collapse___d			It'll	collapsed...
We						We'll	
You						You'll	
They						They'll	

NEGATIVE ⟶ SHORT FORM (1)   SHORT FORM (2)

will + not + have + past
participle...

I					I		I'll	
You					You		You'll	
He					He		He'll	
She	will	not	have	passed...	She	won't	She'll	not have
It					It	have	It'll	passed...
We					We	passed...	We'll	
You					You		You'll	
They					They		They'll	

QUESTION

will   + have + past participle ... ?

	I		
	you		
	he		
Will	she	have	passed ... ?
	it		
	we		
	you		
	they		

USE	**One action will finish before another or before a certain time**

We use this tense to describe a future action which we know
will finish *before* another or before a certain time, which is
described in the present simple. It is often used with adverbs
and adverbial phrases of time, like:

by   before   by the time

By the time she gets dressed the bus **will have** left.

You'**ll have spent** all your money **before** the holiday's over.

You'**ll have entered** the building **by the time** they close the doors.

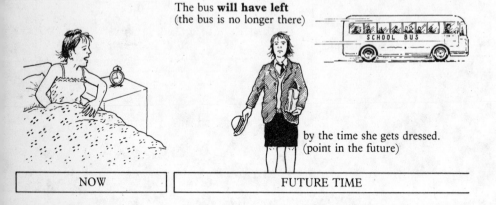

The bus **will have left**
(the bus is no longer there)

by the time she gets dressed.
(point in the future)

NOW	FUTURE TIME

11.31 Future perfect continuous

will have been
striking

The coalminers' strike began ten weeks ago. It has gone on now for longer than any strike in the last five years. By next Monday, June 1st, the miners **will have been striking** for almost eleven weeks.

MINERS' LEADER: We've lasted ten weeks and we'll last another ten if we need to. It's time to make a stand against the government.

─── **form** ───

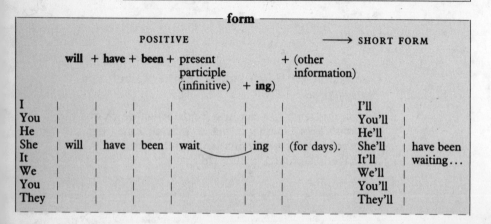

POSITIVE						⟶ SHORT FORM	
will +	**have** +	**been** +	present participle (infinitive) + **ing**)		+ (other information)		
I						I'll	
You						You'll	
He						He'll	
She	will	have	been	wait͜ing		She'll	have been
It					(for days).	It'll	waiting...
We						We'll	
You						You'll	
They						They'll	

NEGATIVE					SHORT FORM (1)		SHORT FORM (2)	
will + not + have + been + present participle								
I					I		I'll	
You					You		You'll	
He					He		He'll	
She	will	not	have	been	waiting	She	won't have	She'll	not have
It					It	been	It'll	been
We					We	waiting	We'll	waiting
You					You		You'll	
They					They		They'll	

QUESTION

will - **+ have + been +** present participle . . . ?

Will	I			
	you			
	he			
	she			
Will	it	have	been	waiting . . . ?
	we			
	you			
	they			

USE

A continuous action finishing by a fixed time in the future

The FUTURE PERFECT CONTINUOUS describes a continuous action (very often one which is already in progress) which will finish *by* a certain point in the future:

In ten minutes we**'ll have been waiting** for this bus for exactly an hour!

Amer **will have been studying** English for ten months by the time he goes home to Syria in October.

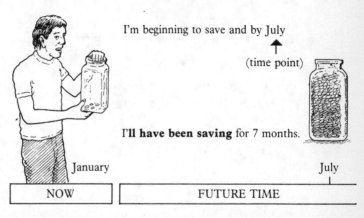

I'm beginning to save and by July

↑
(time point)

I**'ll have been saving** for 7 months.

| January | | July |

| NOW | FUTURE TIME |

11.32   be to (future)

> NEWSCASTER: The strike in the coal industry has now been going on for ten weeks. The Prime Minister referred to it as a disgrace and a scandal that it should happen in modern Britain.
>
> is to be   There **is to be** a meeting tomorrow between the directors of the National Coal Board and the miners'
>
> are to discuss   union. They **are to discuss** possible ways out of this impasse.

---
form

POSITIVE   ⟶ SHORT FORM

present simple + **to** + infinitive + (other
   of **be**   information)

I	am	to	arrange	(transport facilities).	I'm	to arrange...
You	are	to	decide	(without me).	You're	to decide...
He					He's	
She	is	to	arrive	(next month).	She's	to arrive...
It					It's	
We					We're	
You	are	to	encourage	(support).	You're	to encourage...
They					They're	

NEGATIVE   ⟶ SHORT FORM (1)   SHORT FORM (2)

present simple + **not** + **to** + infinitive . . .
   of **be**

I	am	not	to	arrange...	—	I'm	not to arrange...
You	are	not	to	decide...	You aren't to decide...	You're	not to decide...
He					He	He's	
She	is	not	to	arrive...	She isn't to arrive...	She's	not to arrive...
It					It	It's	
We					We	We're	
You	are	not	to	encourage...	You aren't to encourage...	You're	not to encourage...
They					They	They're	

QUESTION

present simple of **be** + **to** + infinitive . . . ?

Am	I	to	arrange . . . ?	
Are	you	to	decide . . . ?	
	he			
Is	she	to	arrive . . . ?	
	it			
	we			
Are	you	to	encourage . . . ?	
	they			

USE **Formal announcements**

We use the **be to** future in more formal language. It is often used in TV, newspaper or radio reports to describe an action which will take place in the future (see above text), or to give formal or impersonal instructions about future events:

You **are to report** to the officer on duty at three p.m.

See also **be** (9.2–9.3).

11.33 Present simple for the future

USE **Future programmes**

The PRESENT SIMPLE (11.3) of many verbs can be used as a future tense in timetables, schedules and other future programmes:

The bus **leaves** at twelve-fifteen exactly.
On Sunday we **leave** London at noon and **arrive** in Edinburgh at one o'clock.

11.34 Bird's eye box: Future tenses

They **are leaving** tomorrow.	⟶ present continuous, definite arrangements
He'll **arrive** later this week.	⟶ **will** future
I'm **going to have** my holiday in Greece next year.	⟶ **going to** future
She'll **be driving** a Jaguar when you see her again.	⟶ future continuous
She'll **have left** before we arrive.	⟶ future perfect
They'll **have been skiing** for several hours by the time we arrive.	⟶ future perfect continuous
The committee **is to discuss** it tomorrow.	⟶ **be to** future
Your first lesson **starts** on Monday at nine a.m.	⟶ simple present, timetables/schedules

12 UNREAL PAST (SUBJUNCTIVE)

CONTENTS   *page*

12.1   Unreal past (**it's time, 'd rather, if only**)   166

12.1.1 **was** or **were**?   167

12.2   Bird's eye box (unreal past (subjunctive))   168

12.1 Unreal past

it's time . . .
decided
I'd rather . . . did

if I were you I'd
it's time . . . grew
up

> '**It's time** you **decided** to do some work, my boy.
> You've wasted a lot of time with sport and entertainment.
> **I'd rather** you **did** something positive about your future.
> When I was your age I had achieved a lot of things.
> **If I were you I'd** really work hard. Your generation is
> lazy. **It's time** you all **grew up**.'
>   This was what my father said on the day I left school.

─────── **form** ───────

special phrase   + (pro)noun (subject)   + past tense

It's time | I | went.
It's high time | we | saved up.
I'd rather | you | explained.
They'd much rather | Paul | drove.

USE   Imagined situations

We use the UNREAL PAST (the SUBJUNCTIVE) to show that
we are imagining an unreal situation. Certain phrases are
followed by a past tense when a present tense might be
expected:

EXPRESSION	EXAMPLE	MEANING
it's time	→ It's time you **washed** your shirt.	→ You should wash your shirt. (opinion)
it's high time	→ It's high time you **learned** how to behave.	→ You should really know how to behave by now. (stronger opinion)
But It's time to wash your shirt.	→	Today is washing day. (statement of fact)

166

EXPRESSION	EXAMPLE	MEANING
'd rather	→ **I'd rather** you **paid** me now.	→ Ideally (in my mind) you would give me the money now. (preference)
if	→ **If** I **had** the time, I'd **go** with you.	→ (see Chapter 19)
if only	→ **If only** I **had** a car.	→ I really want a car. (strong desire)
wish	→ **I wish** you **understood** me.	→ I want you to understand me (but you don't). (desire)
suppose	→ **Suppose** you **were** late?	→ Let's consider the possibility of your being late.
as though	→ I care for him **as though** he **were** my own child.	→ I treat him like my own child.
as if	→ You talk about her **as if** you **hated** her.	→ You seem to hate her.

When we want to say, for example:

I want you to pay me now.
or
I think you should pay me now.

we can use the unreal past:

It's time you **paid** me.

12.1.1 *was* or *were*?

 He looked as if he **were** dead. *or* as if he **was** dead.

In the normal past simple the form is:

I
he
she   **was**
it

When we talk about an imaginary situation the form is:

I
he
she   **were**
it

If I **were** you, I'd buy an umbrella.
If only he **were** here I would be so happy.

In formal written English **were** is always used in the unreal past. In everyday spoken English it is sometimes forgotten, and **was** is used with **I, he, she** and **it**.

See also CONDITIONAL SENTENCES (19.2).

12.2 Bird's eye box: Unreal past (subjunctive)

> it's (high) time
> 'd rather
> if (only)
> wish   + past tense
> suppose
> as though
> as if

13 To + Infinitive

13.1   object + to + infinitive

nothing to do
the kitchen to clean
the dinner to cook,
the shopping to do
a comic to read

> SON: I'm really bored. I've got **nothing to do**.
> MOTHER: You're lucky! I've got **the kitchen to clean**,
>   **the dinner to cook** and **the shopping to do**! Why don't
>   you help me? You could make a cake.
> SON: That's all right. I've just found a **comic to read**!

--- **form** ---

(pro)noun (object) + **to** +   infinitive

a problem	to	discuss
a question	to	answer
them	to	please

USE

To shorten a longer phrase

We have a problem **to** discuss.
⟶ We have a problem which we should discuss.

I've got a comic **to** read.
⟶ I've got a comic which I can read.

We can build sentences in the following way:

		to CONSTRUCTION
There's a room which we should (can) clean.	⟶	We've a room **to** clean.
You've a book which you should (can) read.	⟶	You've a book **to** read.

169

13.2 adjective + to + infinitive

kind to lend
too lazy to walk
good enough to
pay

> CHRIS: You were very **kind to lend** me your bike. I was just **too lazy to walk** all the way to the bank.
>
> IAN: That's all right. Now you can be **good enough to pay** me the money that you owe me.
>
> ――――― **form** ―――――
>
> adjective + to + infinitive
>
> | good | to | swim |
> | certain | to | answer |
> | delighted | to | come |

USE

to + INFINITIVE often follows an adjective:

I'm **ready to go** to school.

NOTE

I'm **eager to please.**
――→ I am very keen to please someone else.

I'm **easy to please.**
――→ It is easy for someone else to please **me**.

This construction is often used after SUPERLATIVE ADJECTIVES (6.6) and expressions with **too** and **enough**:

The examination was **too terrible to talk about.**

13.3 question word + to + infinitive

where to go, what
to do

which to see
whether to choose

> ALEC: I don't know **where to go** or **what to do.**
>
> GEORGE: Why don't you go to the cinema? There are a couple of good films on at the moment.
>
> ALEC: That's another problem. I don't know **which to see**. I don't know **whether to choose** *Star Wars* or *Love Story*.
>
> ――――― **form** ―――――
>
> question word + **to** + infinitive
>
> | who | to | see |
> | which | to | choose |
> | when | to | leave |

USE

We put **to** + INFINITIVE in a clause (4.12. ☞ 2) as an alternative to asking a question. It is less direct:

How can I tell you?
⟶ I don't know **how to tell you**.
not I don't know in what way I should tell you.

When shall I switch on the video?
⟶ I have no idea **when to switch on** the video.

NOTE

Although **whether** is not a question word, we use it in the same way (**whether** + **to** + infinitive) when expressing uncertainty about a choice:

I don't know **whether to buy** the Citroen or the Mercedes.

See also QUESTION WORDS (Chapter 5) and REPORTED QUESTIONS (20 ☞ 5).

13.4 to + infinitive (purpose)

to show you my
new records
to buy a sweater
to buy records

> JILL: Hi, Sally. I've come **to show you my new records**. I went **to buy a sweater**, but then I heard this record playing . . .
> SALLY: I suppose when you go **to buy records** you usually come out of the shop with clothes!

USE

to + INFINITIVE is often used to explain **why** something is done. It can replace the expression **in order to** + INFINITIVE which is much more formal:

I'm going to university **to study politics/in order to study politics**.

13.5 Verbs followed by to + infinitive

try to clean

learn to operate
seems to be
want to know

need to know

> SALESMAN: As you see, when we **try to clean** even the dirtiest part of your carpet there is no problem for this vacuum-cleaner.
> CUSTOMER: But how easily can I **learn to operate** this machine? It **seems to be** extremely complicated to me.
> SALESMAN: If you **want to know** how to get the best out of your new Dirt-Up vacuum cleaner you should read this brochure. It tells you everything you **need to know.**

verb	+ to	+ infinitive	verb	+ to	+ infinitive
agree	to	(come)	intend	to	(meet)
appear	to	(cry)	learn	to	(be)
arrange	to	(stay)	love	to	(travel)
attempt	to	(pass)	need	to	(speak)
begin	to	(laugh)	offer	to	(drive)
decide	to	(leave)	promise	to	(wait)
expect	to	(fail)	refuse	to	(accept)
forget	to	(lock)	seem	to	(understand)
hate	to	(argue)	try	to	(cheat)
help	to	(start)	want	to	(live)
hope	to	(see)	wish	to	(visit)

form

USE

After certain verbs we sometimes make sentences with
to + INFINITIVE (see table above):

David **agreed to pay** for all the damage to the car.

She **appears to be** very nervous but, in fact, she's not.

I always **intended to tell** you but the truth is that I never had the courage.

See also GERUND OR TO + INFINITIVE (15.4).

13.6 Bird's eye box: to + infinitive

We have **a question to answer.**	→ object + to + infinitive
She was **brave to try.**	→ adjective + to + infinitive
He didn't know **where to look.**	→ question word + to + infinitive
I went to the bank **to cash** £100.	→ to + infinitive (purpose)
Mary **offered to type** it.	→ verb followed by to + infinitive

14 INFINITIVE WITHOUT TO

14.1   Modal verbs and modal verb phrases + infinitive

USE

Regular modals

After REGULAR MODALS (10.2–10.24) the main verb is an INFINITIVE WITHOUT **to**:

	modal verb	infinitive without **to**	

The spaceship **should** **land** in ten minutes.

You'd **better drive** slowly or the police **may stop** you.
(modal verb phrase + infinitive without **to**; modal verb + infinitive without **to**)

IRREGULAR MODALS (10.1, 10.25–10.30) are followed by **to** + INFINITIVE (see also Chapter 13):

modal verb — **to** + infinitive

I **need** **to see** you.

modal verb — **to** + infinitive

I **used** **to live** in India.

14.2 make/let + infinitive

let me look

made me buy
make you buy

> WIFE: Oh! You've got the holiday photos. **Let me look** at them, please.
>
> HUSBAND: Yes, they're really much better than our usual photos. I'm glad you **made me buy** a new camera.
>
> WIFE: I didn't exactly **make you buy** it. I just offered advice.

────────────────── form ──────────────────

| make/ | + (pro)noun | + infinitive |
let	(object)	(without **to**)
I made	him	come.
John made	the class	work (harder).
You let	the door	shut.
The teacher let	them	talk.

USE 1

Forcing somebody

We use **make** + INFINITIVE when we want to force or oblige somebody to do something:

Make him **do** as he's told.

Make her **pay back** the money she owes.

Make Jenny **see** sense if you can.

USE 2

let + INFINITIVE has two different meanings:

PERMISSION

Let her **drive** this evening. ⟶ Allow her to drive this evening.

Please **let** me **go** to the party.

MORAL OBLIGATION

Let them **wait** for once. ⟶ They ought to wait for once, because they normally arrive late.

Let him **find out** the hard way.

14.3 Verbs of perception + infinitive

> POLICEMAN: There's been a robbery here. I want to speak to anybody who saw anything at seven o'clock this evening.

saw . . . arrive
noticed . . .
signal . . .
hear . . .
scream/shout
see . . . come
heard . . . shout

MR JACKSON: I was here. I **saw** a car **arrive** at about six o'clock. The driver waited for an hour. Then I **noticed** him **signal** to somebody in the building. Then there was a loud bang inside the building.
POLICEMAN: Did you **hear** anybody **scream** or **shout**? Did you **see** anyone **come** out of the building?
MR JACKSON: I **heard** someone **shout** 'murderer'. Then three men ran out, jumped into the car and drove off.

--- form ---

	verb	+ (pro)noun (object)	+ infinitive (without **to**)
He	saw	the man	jump.
They	heard	her	shout.
I'm	watching	them	run.
She	felt	John	look.

USE

Perceiving/sensing an action

When we use verbs like **see**, **hear**, **watch**, **notice** and **feel** + INFINITIVE we emphasize experience of the *complete* action, from beginning to end:

The policeman **saw** the man **take out** a pistol.
——→ The policeman saw the man put his hand into his pocket *and* take out a pistol.

I **heard** her **tell** the story to the class.
——→ It is clear I heard the whole story.
but
I **heard** her **telling** the story to the class.
——→ It is possible I heard only part of the story.

See also PRESENT PARTICIPLE (AFTER VERBS OF PERCEPTION) (16.1.3).

14.4 Bird's eye box: Infinitive without to

It **may happen**.	——→ modal + infinitive
You'd **better pay** for it.	——→ modal phrase + infinitive
Make him **apologize**.	——→ **make/let** +infinitive
She **saw** me **sign** the cheque.	——→ verb of perception + infinitive

15 THE GERUND

CONTENTS *page*

15.1 Gerund as subject

collecting

watching

watching

eating

> JAMES: In my book it says I have to ask my friends about their hobbies so that I can make a graph.
> MATTHEW: **Collecting** space figures is my favourite hobby and **watching** television is my second.
> JAMES: **Watching** television sounds a bit boring. You must like something else!
> MATTHEW: **Eating** sausages and chips is another of my favourite activities, and you could mention ice-cream.

---
form
---

gerund	+	verb	+ other information
Swimming		keeps	you in good health.
Smoking		is	dangerous.
Sitting here		is getting	very boring.
Parachuting		looks	exciting.
Jogging		sounds	an easy way to keep in shape.

 When we want to form a GERUND, in most cases we take an infinitive and put **ing** on the end:

eat + **ing** ⟶ **Eating** can be a wonderful experience.

sleep + **ing** ⟶ **Sleeping** makes you look younger.

work + **ing** ⟶ **Working** too much can cause a nervous breakdown.

To make a negative gerund we use **not** before it:

Not understanding teenagers is the first sign of middle age!

See SPELLING PRESENT PARTICIPLES (11.1 ☞ 2) for details of spelling rules.

USE

Verbs as nouns

A gerund as the subject of a sentence takes the position in front of the verb:

subject   verb

Cleaning is boring.

Although it is formed from a verb, a gerund behaves like a noun. It can be used with an ARTICLE (see Chapter 3), a DEMONSTRATIVE ADJECTIVE (4.10), a POSSESSIVE ADJECTIVE (4.5), or a PERSONAL PRONOUN (OBJECT) (4.1.1):

The building of private houses is forbidden here.
This shouting is getting on my nerves.
His playing in a band annoys his mother.

His playing can also be the object:

I don't approve of **his playing** in a band. (grammatical but now rather formal)
or
I don't approve of **him playing** in a band. (more natural, everyday English)

15.2 Gerund as object

fancy getting
can't stand
cooking
feel like cooking
suggest trying

> JENNIFER: Do you **fancy getting** some food from a take-away this evening? I really **can't stand cooking** another meal tonight. I'm too tired.
> JOHN: OK. I don't **feel like cooking** either. I **suggest trying** that Chinese take-away in the High Street. It would make a change.

— form —

verb	+ gerund	+ other information
I avoid	using	the tube.
John dislikes	visiting	his aunt.
He's given up	training	at weekends.
We can't stand	smoking.	
The students suggested	going	home early.

After certain verbs

We use a gerund, not an INFINITIVE (see Chapter 13 and 14), after any of the following verbs:

appreciate	fancy	keep	practise
avoid	feel like	keep on	put off
consider	finish	leave off	risk
deny	give up	mind	can't stand
dislike	can't help	miss	suggest
enjoy	imagine	postpone	understand
excuse			

John	**put off**	**paying**	his bill until it was too late.
She	**felt like**	**giving up**	her job.
I	**finished**	**working**	at five o'clock.
	Keep	**trying**	and you'll eventually succeed.

 There are also several verbal phrases after which we use a gerund:

it's no good	it's worth
it's no use	it's not worth

It's no use hoping for a miracle.
It's not worth selling your car. You won't get anything for it.

15.3 Gerund after prepositions or adverbs

of working
on doing
by resting

to working

The farmer had been sleeping in the field for about an hour. He was tired **of working**. In fact he had never been keen **on doing** anything at all at midday when the sun was hottest. **By resting** a little at this time he would be able to do more in the afternoon. Anyway, he wasn't used **to working** more than four hours at a time. Suddenly he woke up. He looked over towards the trees. His heart began to beat in fear . . .

─────── form ───────

	preposition/adverb	+ gerund
I'm tired	of	waiting.
He's exhausted	from	arguing.
They're	in	training.

USE	When we follow a PREPOSITION (**in, on,** etc.) (see Chapter 21) or with a verb, we use a gerund:

The policeman is interested **in catching** the thief.

I'm thinking **of moving** to another country.
Don't worry **about not having** any money. It'll be all right.
You were responsible **for losing** the football match.

15.4   Gerund or to + infinitive (same meaning)

like having
start to rain
like staying

prefer to do
can't bear having

JOHN: How about coming for a picnic today? We could go to the lake.
MARY: I **like having** picnics but I'm afraid it will **start to rain** as soon as we get there. Look at the clouds.
JOHN: Well, I really don't **like staying** in on Sundays. It's so boring.
MARY: I **prefer to do** something active at the weekend too but I **can't bear having** picnics in the rain!

――――――――― **form** ―――――――――

verb	+ gerund	*or*	verb		+ **to**	+ infinitive
It continued	raining.		It continued	|	to |	rain.
I hate	waiting.		I hate	|	to |	wait.

After certain verbs

After the following verbs we can form sentences with a gerund or **to** + INFINITIVE (see Chapter 13):

begin	continue	intend	prefer
can't bear	fear (old-fashioned)	like	propose
cease	hate	love	start

They **began fighting**.	*or* They **began to fight**.
James **can't bear relaxing**.	*or* James **can't bear to relax**.
We **intended going** to the Canary Islands.	*or* We **intended to go** to the Canary Islands.
It will **start raining**.	*or* It will **start to rain**.

Both versions of each sentence mean practically the same.

Verbs after *would*

hate, **love**, **like**, **prefer**, etc.

When these verbs follow **would** (**'d**), **to** + INFINITIVE and *not* the gerund is normally used:

I **would hate to leave** the restaurant without paying.
not
I would hate leaving . . .
Jean'**d like to go** skiing but she hasn't got the money.
We **would like to help** but we haven't got time.
I'**d prefer to keep** myself to myself.

15.5   Gerund or to + infinitive (different meaning)

remember
locking
remember to do
stop worrying

forget to lock
try to think

> MOTHER: Terry, I'm just wondering. I don't **remember locking** the front door of the house. Did you **remember to do** it?
> TERRY: **Stop worrying** about it now! It's too late! Anyway, there's nothing worth stealing.
> MOTHER: I always **forget to lock** the door. I really must **try to think** about it next time.

────────────── **form** ──────────────

verb   + gerund   *and*   verb   + **to**   + infinitive

He stopped	eating.	He stopped	to	eat.
She tried	running.	She tried	to	run.

USE

After certain verbs

After some verbs the incorrect choice of a gerund or **to** + INFINITIVE (see Chapter 13) produces an unintended meaning:

go on	remember	forget	propose	stop	try

The car **went on rolling** even after they had put the brake on.
Try checking the fuses.
Don't **forget to bring** some change with you for the machine.
I never **remember to telephone** my mother at the weekend.

EXAMPLES	MEANING	
a The driver **went on driving** dangerously even after the police had warned him.	→ The driver continued to drive dangerously.	→ continue an action
b The tennis star won the semi-final and then **went on to win** the final.	→ He won the semi-final and then, afterwards, won the final.	→ proceed to another (later) phase
a I **remembered* seeing** the film before.	→ I remembered that I had seen the film before.	→ remember that something happened in the past
b I **remembered to put** my passport in my pocket.	→ I remembered that I had to put my passport in my pocket.	→ remember that we need to do something

*The opposite of **remember** + GERUND is **not remember** + GERUND. The opposite of
remember + **to** + INFINITIVE is either **not remember** + **to** + INFINITIVE or
forget + **to** + INFINITIVE.

a I **propose* setting up** an inquiry.	→ I suggest an inquiry is set up.	→ suggest an action
b I **propose to speak** to the chairman about it.	→ I (personally) intend to speak to the chairman about it.	→ state an intention

*It is also common to say: I propose (that) we (should) . . .

a Paul **stopped smoking**.	→ Paul did not smoke any longer.	→ no longer do something
b Paul **stopped to light** a cigarette.	→ Paul stopped in order to light it (because he wanted to light it).	→ stop for a purpose
a **Try going** to work by public transport.	→ Make an experiment and go to work by public transport.	→ try a strategy
b **Try to be** on time tomorrow.	→ Make an effort to be on time tomorrow.	→ try something difficult

NOTE Basically most infinitive constructions suggest something ahead, a future idea. Gerund constructions do not necessarily do so (they can refer to a more general idea).

15.6 Bird's eye box: The gerund

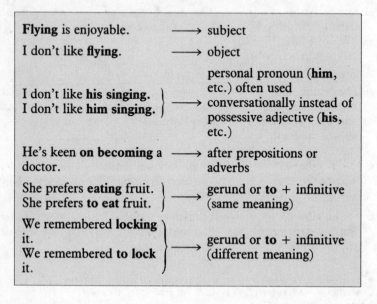

Flying is enjoyable.	⟶ subject
I don't like **flying**.	⟶ object
I don't like **his singing**. I don't like **him singing**.	⟶ personal pronoun (**him**, etc.) often used conversationally instead of possessive adjective (**his**, etc.)
He's keen **on becoming** a doctor.	⟶ after prepositions or adverbs
She prefers **eating** fruit. She prefers **to eat** fruit.	⟶ gerund or **to** + infinitive (same meaning)
We remembered **locking** it. We remembered **to lock** it.	⟶ gerund or **to** + infinitive (different meaning)

16 PARTICIPLES

16.1 Present participle (as adjective)

banging

JIM: That **banging** door is getting on my nerves. I haven't slept at all tonight. I might as well get up and make a cup of tea.

interesting

JEAN: That's an **interesting** idea. You could close the door at the same time.

flashing

JIM: Oh! What's that **flashing** light over there? My goodness! It's a police car. What do they want?

burning

POLICEMAN (*at the door*): Sorry to disturb you, sir, but have you noticed a strong **burning** smell? I'm afraid your garage has already burned to the ground!

--- **form** ---

(article/quantifier)	+ participle	+ noun (singular/plural)
—	shocking	news
a	tiring	journey
some	interesting	ideas

183

(pro)noun (subject)	+ be (or some other verbs)	+ participle
It	is	exciting.
The news	sounds	alarming.
She	looks	appealing.

We form a PRESENT PARTICIPLE by adding **ing** to an infinitive:

burn + **ing** ⟶ the **burning** house
exhaust + **ing** ⟶ an **exhausting** race

When an infinitive ends with **e** we leave this letter out:

love ⟶ a **loving** wife

For complete spelling rules refer to SPELLING PRESENT PARTICIPLES (11.1 ☞ 2).

USE 1

In front of nouns

We can use a present participle in front of a NOUN (see Chapter 2) in order to give extra information about it as an ADJECTIVE does (6.1).

USE 2

After *be*

We can use a present participle to give extra information about a noun when we put the participle after the verb **be** (9.2.3–9.3), exactly like an ADJECTIVE (6.2).

We can also use present participles predicatively, after certain verbs, exactly like ADJECTIVES (6.2 ☞).

The most common present participles as adjectives are:

amazing	exciting	shocking
amusing	frightening	surprising
confusing	interesting	tiring
embarrassing	pleasing	worrying

The **amazing** thing about the whole situation was that they were able to live for so long without water.
What an **interesting** book that was.

16.1.1 Present participle (introducing an adjectival phrase)

standing

lying
running

containing

> FORESTER: Do you see those pine trees **standing** to the right of us? The whitish-looking ones with no leaves.
> TOURIST: Yes. Why do they look different from all the others?
> FORESTER: The leaves **lying** on the ground give us the answer. And the little insects **running** around all over the tree trunks will kill off the trees here. Within the next six months you will be standing in a graveyard **containing** only a few rotten tree trunks.
> TOURIST: Can't the authorities do anything about it?

USE

With or without relative pronoun

We can use a present participle to introduce an adjectival phrase (see Chapter 6 for ADJECTIVES), in order to give extra information about a NOUN (see Chapter 2). The phrase may or may not include a RELATIVE PRONOUN (4.12):

adjectival phrase
participle
The man **swimming through the water** is my uncle.

relative pronoun
⟶ The man **who is swimming through the water** is my uncle.

adjectival phrase
participle
The train **arriving on platform four** is one hour late.

relative pronoun
⟶ The train **which is arriving on platform four** is one hour late.

16.1.2 Present participle (introducing an adverbial phrase)

shouting, waving

laughing

concentrating

> **Shouting** loudly and **waving** his arms, the fat shopkeeper ran down the road. A few feet in front of him a small, thin man was sprinting away. **Laughing** loudly, he shouted back to the shopkeeper: 'You'll never catch me. You'll never get your money back.' **Concentrating** on his conversation with the shopkeeper, the thief had not noticed the small boy playing with his roller skates.

bending

> **Bending** quickly, the boy unstrapped a skate and rolled it in front of the man. The thief put his foot on to it and fell flat on his back with a bang.

USE

Showing *how*, *why* or *when*

We can use a present participle to introduce an adverbial phrase (see Chapter 7 for ADVERBS), which answers the question **how?**, **why?** or **when?**:

adverbial phrase

participle

Jane ate her dinner **sitting in front of the television**.
——→ Jane ate her dinner while she sat in front of the television.

adverbial phrase

participle

The footballer, **turning awkwardly**, sprained his ankle.
——→ The footballer sprained his ankle because he turned awkwardly.

16.1.3 Present participle (after verbs of perception)

watched . . .
sailing, listened . . .
singing
felt . . .
rolling

noticed . . .
coming

> JANE: One lunchtime Jim and I left the office and went right down to the harbour. It was lovely. We **watched** boats **sailing** by and **listened** to the birds **singing**.
> SALLY: Weren't you worried that you'd be late back?
> JANE: Not at all. We even paddled and **felt** the cool water **rolling** over our feet! It was idyllic.
> SALLY: Very romantic! But what happened? Did you get back on time?
> JANE: Not quite, but fortunately nobody **noticed** us **coming** in.

form

verb + (pro)noun (object)	+ participle
I saw | you	| going (to the police station today).
He's (often) heard | them	| laughing and joking (in the next room).
They watched | the athletes	| running.
We noticed | her	| smoking.
She felt | him	| looking (at her).

186

USE

Perceiving/sensing an action

When we use a present participle after verbs like **see**, **hear**, **watch**, **notice** and **feel** we emphasize experience of *part* of an action:

I watched the boats **sailing** by.

When we want to emphasize experience of the *complete* action we use an INFINITIVE WITHOUT **to** (14.3) after the verb of perception:

I watched the boats **sail** by.

16.2 Bird's eye box: Present participle

They saw a **sinking** ship.	⟶ as adjective
They saw a ship **sinking** in the harbour.	⟶ introducing an adjectival phrase
Turning over in the water, the ship sank.	⟶ introducing an adverbial phrase
I **saw** it **sinking**.	⟶ after verbs of perception

16.3 Past participle (as adjective)

smashed, broken
uneaten

ruined

disgusted

> CHARLES: I've said this before, I know, but look at this flat. It really is the last time we have a party here! There are four **smashed** glasses and three **broken** plates and there seem to be bits of **uneaten** food everywhere.
> DAVID: You're right – and look at the rug. It's **ruined**. There's red wine all over it.
> MARTIN: Come on – stop feeling so **disgusted**. We'd better get on and clean the place up.

---
form

(article/ quantifier)	+ participle	+ noun (singular/plural)
—	cracked	cups
some	excited	fans
an	expected	victory

(pro)noun (subject) +	be (or some other verbs)	+ participle
The picture	is	damaged.
He	sounds	interested.
The victims	remained	forgotten.

  We form a regular PAST PARTICIPLE by adding **ed** to an infinitive. If an infinitive ends with **e** we add **d** only:

destroy + **ed** ⟶ the **destroyed** city
hate + **d** ⟶ the **hated** ruler

Irregular past participles are formed by changing infinitives in other ways. See PAST SIMPLE (11.11) and 16.3.1.

USE 1 — In front of nouns

We can also use a past participle in front of a NOUN (see Chapter 2) in order to give extra information about it, as an ADJECTIVE does (6.1).

USE 2 — After *be*

We can use a PAST PARTICIPLE to give extra information about a noun when we put the participle after the verb **be** (9.2.3–9.3), exactly like an ADJECTIVE (6.2).

We can also use past participles predicatively, after certain verbs, exactly like ADJECTIVES (6.2 ☞).

NOTE	The plane that made an emergency landing was **damaged**.

In this sentence, **damaged** describes the *state* or *condition* of the aeroplane. It is an adjective and not the PASSIVE (see Chapter 17). The passive describes *actions* not states.

16.3.1 Common irregular past participles

 We cannot use all verbs to form past participle adjectives. Below is a list of the most common irregular verbs which can be put in front of nouns:

beat	⟶ beaten	hurt	⟶ hurt
bend	⟶ bent	knit	⟶ knitted
bind	⟶ bound	know	⟶ known
bite	⟶ bitten	light	⟶ lit
break	⟶ broken	lose	⟶ lost
burn	⟶ burnt	make	⟶ made
burst	⟶ burst	misunderstand	⟶ misunderstood
choose	⟶ chosen	read	⟶ read
drink	⟶ drunk	speak	⟶ spoken
eat	⟶ eaten	spill	⟶ spilt
fall	⟶ fallen	spoil	⟶ spoilt
forbid	⟶ forbidden	steal	⟶ stolen
forget	⟶ forgotten	swell	⟶ swollen
freeze	⟶ frozen	tear	⟶ torn
grind	⟶ ground	weave	⟶ woven
hide	⟶ hidden		

16.3.2 Past participle (introducing an adjectival phrase)

deserted hit destroyed left shocked	The town, almost **deserted** since the battles with the enemy, stood black and half-ruined. Many houses, **hit** and **destroyed** by bombs and gun-fire, were nothing more than piles of stones. There were still a few people **left** amongst the buildings. Now, after the soldiers had gone away, they were beginning to creep out. **Shocked** by what they saw around, they stood silently.

With or without relative pronoun

We can use a past participle to introduce an adjectival phrase (see Chapter 6 for ADJECTIVES), in order to give extra information about a NOUN (see Chapter 2). The phrase may or may not include a RELATIVE PRONOUN (4.12):

adjectival phrase

participle

The town, **deserted since the battles,** stood black and half-ruined.

relative pronoun

⟶ The town, **which had been deserted since the battles,** stood black and half-ruined.

adjectival phrase

participle

There were still a few people **left amongst the buildings.**

relative pronoun

⟶ There were still a few people **who had been left amongst the buildings.**

Ray, **depressed** after his unfortunate road accident, decided to go for a holiday.

16.4 Perfect participle (introducing an adverbial phrase)

Showing *how*, *why*, or *when*

having + PAST PARTICIPLE can introduce an adverbial phrase (see Chapter 7 for ADVERBS) which answers the question **how?**, **why?** or **when?**:

190

adverbial phrase

participle

Having signed the will, I left the office.
⟶ When I had signed the will, I left the office.

adverbial phrase

participle

Having shown the official my passport, I was allowed to pass.
⟶ Because (*or* After) I had shown the official my passport, I was allowed to pass.

 In everyday language we more often use a LINKING WORD (see Chapter 23) like **before, after, because, when** or **as soon as** followed by the PAST PERFECT (11.22–11.23).

Contrast	
EVERYDAY SPOKEN FORM	MORE FORMAL, WRITTEN FORM
I failed the exam because I hadn't studied.	⟶ Not having studied, I failed the exam.
When she left, she found she had forgotten her purse.	⟶ Having left, she found she had forgotten her purse.

16.5   Bird's eye box: Past/perfect participles

She picked up the **broken** glass.	⟶	as adjective (past participle)
She picked up the glass **broken by** the waiter.	⟶	introducing an adjectival phrase (past participle)
Having broken the glass, the waiter smiled.	⟶	introducing an adverbial phrase (perfect participle)

17 THE PASSIVE

CONTENTS

17.1 Passive (general)

are sold
are built, are
produced
were . . . sold
is said
are exported
are not . . .
constructed
are . . . finished

Mini motor cars **are sold** all over Europe. Most of these cars **are built** in Great Britain where they **are produced** in the Midlands and the North. Last year 100,000 Minis **were** actually **sold** in this country and 50,000 abroad.

Unfortunately, it **is said** that there is a poor 'after sales' service for British cars which **are exported** abroad. Many people say that the cars **are not** well **constructed** and **are** often badly **finished**.

───── **form** ─────

subject	+ **be**	+ past participle	+ extra information
A car	is	sold	every day.
A note	was	written	yesterday.
It	is	said	that they are not good.
John	was	asked	the question.
They	were	given	a chance.

USE

Formal

The PASSIVE is used when formal or impersonal language is required:

Newspaper articles The Princess **can be seen** with her new baby in her arms.

Scientific writing	When the liquid **is heated** it evaporates.
Notices	Dogs **must be kept** on a lead.
	Smoking **is not allowed**.

We can make a contrast between two types of sentence:

 1 Active/passive contrast

Contrast

ACTIVE		⟶		PASSIVE	
subject +	verb +	object	new subject +	verb	+ agent
1	2	3	3	2	1
I	read	the book. ⟶	The book	was read	by me.
He	wrote	the letter. ⟶	The letter	was written	by him.

 2 Active into passive

We use the following procedure to change a sentence from the active into the passive:

 1   2   3

ACTIVE The thief stole the money.

1 We put the object (3) at the beginning of the passive sentence, where it becomes the subject.

2 The subject (1) becomes the agent and stands at the end of the sentence after **by** or is omitted entirely (see 17.3)

3 The verb is in the PAST SIMPLE (11.11–11.13), so we use the past simple of **be** followed by the PAST PARTICIPLE (16.3 ☞) of the active verb.

3	2	1
PASSIVE The money	was stolen	by the thief.
(new subject)	(past of **be** + past participle of **steal**)	(agent)

 3 These three stages are the same for *all* tenses. The rules concerning tenses in the active and passive are exactly the same (see Chapter 11 for TENSES OF THE VERB (ACTIVE)).

17.2 Different tenses of the passive

	subject	+ **be**	+ past participle*	+ extra information
PRESENT SIMPLE	This office	is	used	every day.
PAST SIMPLE	The decorating	was	finished	last week.
PRESENT PERFECT	The window	has been	broken.	
PAST PERFECT	The window	had been	broken	before I arrived.
FUTURE	The prisoner	will be	shot	tomorrow.
Continuous tenses PRESENT CONTINUOUS	They	are being	introduced	to the boss.
PAST CONTINUOUS	She	was being	offered	the job when I came in.

*See list of common irregular past participles, pages 242–5.

17.3 by + agent

 When do we use **by** + AGENT and when can we leave it out?

A   This type of bread is baked every week.
B   This type of bread is baked by Mr Smith, the wholefood baker.

Sometimes it is not necessary to include **by** + AGENT. It can be left out, as in A above. In B we want to say specifically *who* baked the bread.

The money was stolen.

⟶ We do not know who stole it but, obviously, anyone who steals is a thief.

17.3.1 with

Contrast
The meat was cut by the soldiers.   The meat was cut with a knife.

by tells us who did the action. Here the soldiers cut the meat. **with** tells us what instrument they used. It means 'by means of' or 'with the help of'.

The floor was cleaned **with** a new machine.

NOTE | **Word order**

                    1   2
The book was typed **by** Mary **with** a new typewriter.

17.4 Bird's eye box: Passive (general)

ACTIVE		PASSIVE
The policeman arrested him.	⟶	He **was arrested** (by the policeman).
I'll drive the bus.	⟶	The bus **will be driven** by me.
Michelangelo made the statue using a hammer and chisel.	⟶	The statue was made **by** Michelangelo **with** a hammer and chisel.

17.5 Modal passives

It is possible to make passive sentences with the MODAL VERBS and MODAL VERB PHRASES (see Chapter 10):

ACTIVE		PASSIVE
They **will pay** you later. (active infinitive without **to**)	⟶	You **will be paid** later. (passive infinitive without **to**)
They **ought to pay** teachers more money. (active infinitive with **to**)	⟶	Teachers **ought to be paid** more money. (passive infinitive with **to**)

USE | As the passive is both formal and impersonal it is not often used in conversation. When you want to avoid using it you can use the GENERAL PRONOUNS **one** and **you** (4.2):

You can find the rules of the road in the Highway Code. (informal) **One** can find the rules of the road in the Highway Code. (formal)	⟶ The rules of the road **can be found** in the Highway Code.

17.6   Passive infinitive

to be operated

to be read

> FOREMAN: OK. You three men are new in the factory so I'll explain how this machinery works. The notice on top of the machine says '**To be operated** only by trained personnel.' This means that only men with special permission can use the machine. It also says that there are handbooks on how to use this machinery which are **to be read** carefully before you begin.

---
form

to + **be** + past participle

(This picture is)   to | be | carried   (with care).

(My office is not)   to | be | used   (while I'm away).

USE

Formal instructions

The PASSIVE INFINITIVE can be similar in meaning to **must** and **have to** (10.19–10.20). It is often used for giving orders and formal instructions.

Dogs are **to be kept** on a lead.
⟶ You must keep your dog on a lead.

These tablets are **to be dissolved** in water before they are taken.
⟶ You have to dissolve these tablets in water before you take them.

17.7   Bird's eye box: Modal passives/Passive infinitive

He **must be given** a prize.
He **ought to be congratulated.** } ⟶ modal passives

The door is **to be locked.**   ⟶ passive infinitive

18 QUESTION TAGS

CONTENTS

18.1 Question tags (general)

. . . do you?

. . . do I?

. . . hasn't it?

. . . was I?

. . . don't we?

> JANICE: You've come home early today. You don't feel sick or something, **do you**?
>
> JOHN: I'm not sick at all. I don't look ill, **do I**? In fact I'm feeling better than I've done for a long time.
>
> JANICE: So why are you home from work so early? Something's happened, **hasn't it**? What is it?
>
> JOHN: I've given up my job, actually. Look, I wasn't getting anywhere, **was I**? I'll try to get a better one in the next couple of weeks.
>
> JANICE: But we need money to live, **don't we**? What are we going to live on?

--- **form** ---

	positive verb	+	negative tag
I	met	you at Peter's,	didn't I?
You	were	still at school then,	weren't you?

	negative verb	+	positive tag
He	won't come,	on the train,	will he?
They	weren't		were they?

| USE |

To get confirmation

When we ask a direct question it is to get specific information:

Do you eat fish? ——→ Yes, I do.

Sometimes, however, we want to ask a question to which we already know the answer – or we think we know the answer. In such cases, we make a statement and add a QUESTION TAG:

You enjoyed that meal, **didn't you**?
John will be arriving by train, **won't he**?

197

We usually use question tags when we expect the person we are addressing to agree with us. It isn't a genuine question:

It's a lovely day, **isn't it?**

⟶ We can *see* the weather is nice; we simply want to make conversation about it.

18.2 Forming question tags

There are two ways of forming question tags.

A When the verb in the main sentence is positive the tag is *negative*:

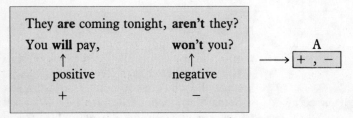

B When the verb in the main sentence is negative the tag is *positive*:

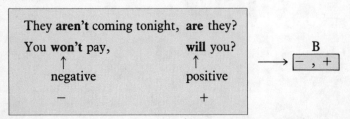

Type A

MAIN SENTENCE	QUESTION TAG	POSSIBLE ANSWERS
The man **is** holding a book,	**isn't** he?	⟶ Yes, he **is.** / No, he **isn't.**
She **wants** to leave,	**doesn't** she?	⟶ Yes, she **does.** / No, she **doesn't.**
You **will** drive me there,	**won't** you?	⟶ Yes, I **will.** / No, I **won't.**

198

Type B

MAIN SENTENCE	QUESTION TAG	POSSIBLE ANSWERS
The building **isn't** closed,	**is** it?	⟶ **Yes**, it **is**. **No**, it **isn't**.
She **doesn't** speak Japanese,	**does** she?	⟶ **Yes**, she **does**. **No**, she **doesn't**.
We **didn't** come late,	**did** we?	⟶ **Yes**, you **did**. **No**, you **didn't**.
You **couldn't** understand it,	**could** you?	⟶ **Yes**, we **could**. **No**, we **couldn't**.

18.2.1 Which verb to use

 A question tag repeats the AUXILIARY (9.2.3) or MODAL (10.1) in the main sentence. If there is no auxiliary (as is the case in a positive statement in the PRESENT SIMPLE (11.3) or PAST SIMPLE (11.11) we use **do**, **does** or did (9.4.1–9.4.2):

They **live** in London, **don't** they?
She **wears** beautiful clothes, **doesn't** she?
John **worked** in a bank, **didn't** he?

NOTE

1 be

I'm absolutely right, **aren't** I? ⟶ *not* **amn't** I?

2 Names

Names are never repeated in tags. The PERSONAL PRONOUN (SUBJECT) (4.1) is always used:

Alan often comes to school late, doesn't **he**?

18.3 Tone of voice

 When we use a question tag only to ask for agreement from another person (that is, when we are sure they will agree with us and will be very surprised if they don't), we use a falling

↘ tone on the tag:

He lives in Egypt, **doesn't he?** (voice drops at the end)
⟶ I'm sure he lives in Egypt.

199

This is the most common way of using a tag.

But we sometimes use a tag to show extreme surprise, or when we are unsure of our information but don't want to ask a direct question to check it.

Then we use a rising ↗ tone on the tag:

You don't like English beer, **do you?** ↘ ↗
⟶ I'm surprised you like English beer.

He lives in Egypt, **doesn't he?** ↘ ↗ (voice rises at the end)
⟶ I think he might live in Egypt but I'm not at all sure.

18.4 Bird's eye box: Question tags

+ , − The car **is** broken, **isn't it?**	⟶ positive sentence, negative tag
− , + The car **isn't** broken, **is it?**	⟶ negative sentence, positive tag
They **came** late, **didn't they?**	⟶ positive sentence in present simple or past simple, negative tag with **do/does/did**
He **might come, mightn't he?**	⟶ modal tags
She lived in Brazil once, didn't she? ↗ ↘	⟶ falling tone to ask for agreement
You can't really eat all that, can you? ↘ ↗	⟶ rising tone to show surprise
James Joyce wrote *Ulysses*, didn't he? ↘ ↗	⟶ rising tone to check information we are unsure of

19 CONDITIONAL SENTENCES

CONTENTS

19.1 First conditional

if . . . moves, . . .
'll shoot

> BANK ROBBER: OK, everybody! Be very quiet. Don't move. **If anybody moves, I'll shoot** them. You there, clerk! Where's the money?
> BANK CLERK: We don't keep any large sums of money here in the building.

if . . .
don't tell . . . ,
. . . 'll shoot

> BANK ROBBER: You're lying. I know it's here. **If you don't tell** me, **I'll shoot** you. I haven't got any time to argue.

if . . . look . . . ,
. . . 'll find

> BANK CLERK: OK. **If you look** in this drawer, you'll **find** the number for the combination of the safe.

if . . . 's . . . ,
. . . 'll be

> BANK ROBBER: That's better. But **if it's** the wrong number, you'll **be** sorry.

———— form ————

if + present simple +, + **will** future

If	I take	an umbrella ,	it won't rain.
If	I have	time ,	I'll visit her.

USE

Future condition – likely

If X happens, (then) Y will happen.
If it rains,   (then) I will get wet.

We use CONDITIONAL SENTENCES when we wish to link two events. The second of these is dependent on the first. When we are fairly certain that the first event will take place we use the FIRST CONDITIONAL.

It is possible to reverse the clauses without changing the meaning: I will get wet if it rains.

In this case there is no comma between them.

1 Conditional linking words

The **if** (conditional) clause can begin with several words besides **if**:

> if   unless (if . . . not)   in case   as long as
> supposing   provided that   so long as

In this clause we use the present tense and *not* the future:

He'll be safe **as long as** he **doesn't** get nervous.
not
He'll be safe as long as he **won't** get nervous.

You will have to work hard **unless** you **want** to fail the test.

I'll take an umbrella **in case** it **rains**.

2 We can also use this form with the IMPERATIVE (11.9) instead of the future tense:

Take an umbrella in case it rains!
Buy me a magazine if you see one I like.

19.2 Second conditional

if . . . lived . . .
. . . would grow
'd be able to . . .
'd learn

if . . . lived . . .
. . .'d be sneezing

> PETE: I really hate my flat in the centre of town. **If I
> lived** in the country, **I would grow** all my own
> vegetables and **I'd be able to** walk for miles in total
> peace. **I'd learn** about birds and trees and . . .
> JEN: Come on, be realistic! You never walk if you can
> help it and what's more you're allergic to grass! **If you
> lived** in the country, you'**d be sneezing** all day!

──────── **form** ────────

if	+ past simple	+ , +	**would**	+ infinitive
If	I married	her ,	I'd	be rich.
If	it wasn't	so late ,	I'd	go.

USE

Future condition – unlikely

With this type of conditional sentence we are imagining an
unlikely situation (see 12.1 for UNREAL PAST):

If I **lived** in the country, I **would grow** all my own vegetables.

The speaker is imagining living in the country. In fact he does
not live there and does not really *expect* to.

If I lived in the country, I |would| grow all my own vegetables.
                            |could|

The difference between the first and second conditionals is that the second deals with events which are extremely unlikely to occur and sometimes totally impossible:

If I'm the Prime Minister, I'll reduce taxes. (first conditional)

The speaker is a political party leader on the eve of a general election.

If I **were** the Prime Minister, I'**d** reduce taxes. (second conditional)

The speaker is an ordinary citizen criticizing the Prime Minister of his country.

If the weather **stays** fine, we'**ll** go to the beach. (first conditional)

It sounds as if the sun is shining so going to the beach is quite likely.

If the weather **stayed** fine, we'**d** go to the beach. (second conditional)

The weather is doubtful and the trip to the beach sounds unlikely.

Supposing he **loses** his job, what **will** he do? (first conditional)

Supposing he **lost** his job, what **would** he do? (second conditional)

19.2.1 Second conditional – *was* or *were*

(See 12.1.1 for UNREAL PAST.)

In the conditional (if) clause of the second conditional we use the past simple. If the verb is **be** the form is usually **were**:

If he **were** here, we could solve the problem immediately.
not
If he **was** here, . . .

If it **were** left to me, I would give you the money.
not
If it **was** left to me, . . .

If I **were** you, I'd go to bed early.
not
If I **was** you, . . .

In everyday spoken English **I**, **he**, **she** and **it** are *sometimes* followed by **was**:

If I **was** three years older, I'd join the army.

but it is safer to use **were** in all more formal situations and in business letter writing.

19.3   Third conditional

if . . . had realized
. . . , . . . would
have worked
if . . . had taken
. . . , . . . wouldn't
have done

If Chris **had realized** how difficult it would be to get a job later, he **would have worked** much harder at school. But he didn't realize. Anyway, nobody explained it to him. Even **if** his teachers **had taken** the trouble to help him, Chris **wouldn't have done** anything. He was only interested in playing tennis when he was at school.

Now Chris has a job repairing broken tennis racquets!

form

if + past perfect	**+, + would**	+ perfect infinitive (have + past participle)

| If | you had run | faster , | you would | have won. |
| If | he hadn't found | water , | he would | have died. |

USE

Past condition – now impossible

The third conditional is used for talking about something which has already happened and so is actually impossible to change:

ANDY: **If** our goalkeeper **hadn't been injured**, we **would have won**.

BRIAN: Yes, and if we'**d scored** another goal, we **could have won** the cup.

The goalkeeper *was* injured, and they *didn't* score another goal.

UNREALITY	FACT
Supposing he had learned to swim, he wouldn't have drowned.	He didn't learn to swim and he drowned.
If you had put some petrol in the car, it wouldn't have stopped.	You didn't put any petrol in the car and it stopped.

19.4 Bird's eye box: Conditional sentences

If he **drinks,** he **will have** an accident. (first conditional)	⟶ future condition – likely
If you **go** to the pub, **don't drink** too much. (first conditional)	⟶ with imperative (orders)
If he **drank,** he **would have** an accident. (second conditional)	⟶ future condition – unlikely
If I **were** younger, I **would dance** all night. (second conditional)	⟶ with **be**
If he **had driven,** he **would have had** an accident. (third conditional)	⟶ past condition – impossible

20 INDIRECT (REPORTED) SPEECH

20.1   Indirect speech introduced by present tense

says that . . . are leaving

says that . . . wants

's . . . complaining that . . . is

JOHN: Hey, Mario. I've just been talking to Chris. He **says that** he and his wife **are leaving** to live in Africa – for ever.

MARIO: Oh! When do they want to go?

JOHN: Chris **says that** he **wants** to leave next week – as soon as possible.

MARIO: Oh well, it's probably the best thing he could do. He's always **complaining that** the climate **is** too cold here.

---
form
---

present tense

They	tell me	(that) I'm wrong.
He	says	(that) it's too cold.
She	says	(that) they were very rich.

USE

Immediate reporting

We can report the words of another person by introducing the INDIRECT (or REPORTED) SPEECH with a PRESENT TENSE verb (11.1–11.6). When we do this the tense of the indirect speech is the same as that of the DIRECT SPEECH.

DIRECT SPEECH	INDIRECT SPEECH
(words of the original speaker)	present

JOHN: I**'ve got** a new job. ⟶ John **says** (that) he**'s got** a new job.

ETHEL: Kathryn **will be** late ⟶ Ethel **says** (that) Kathryn **will be** late
today.   today.

A present tense introduction is used when reporting
immediately; for instance, during or *just after* a telephone
conversation or while reading a letter and passing on some of
the information to another person.

 that

When we report somebody's words we can include the word
that or we can leave it out. It is more formal to include it:

He says **that** you are wrong. (formal)
He says you are wrong. (informal)

20.2   Indirect speech introduced by past tense

warned . . .	Renault, the French automobile manufacturer, **warned**
that . . . could	yesterday **that** a strike at one of its factories **could**
endanger	**endanger** production of the new Super Renault 5. A
said that . . .	spokesman for the company **said that** the car **would be**
would be launched	**launched** on Friday of the following week.
reported that . . .	It was **reported that** a strike at the Renault factory **had**
had . . . stopped	already **stopped** all production. Pickets at the factory
announced that . . .	**announced that** they **would prevent** workers from
would prevent	entering the factory.
commented . . .	Management at Renault **commented** early this morning
that . . . might	**that** a serious strike **might cost** workers their jobs.
cost	From the *Financial Times*, Saturday, 22 September 1984

───────── **form** ─────────

He said (that) he could win.
She said (that) she wanted to play.
We said (that) we'd heard it before.

USE	**Delayed reporting**

We introduce indirect speech with a past tense verb when we want to report somebody's words after they have said them. The tense of the indirect speech is not the same as that of the direct speech:

DIRECT SPEECH	INDIRECT SPEECH
(words of original speaker)	past
	↓
JOHN: **I'm going** to dinner. ⟶	John **said** (that) he **was going** to dinner.
SHEILA: Jane **wants** to visit Egypt. ⟶	Sheila **said** (that) Jane **wanted** to visit Egypt.

20.3 Converting direct speech into indirect speech

 1 Different tenses

DIRECT SPEECH	INDIRECT SPEECH
	He said (that) . . .
'I'm **eating** an apple.'	⟶ he **was eating** an apple.
'I **eat** apples every day.'	⟶ he **ate** apples every day.
'I **ate** an apple yesterday.'	⟶ he **had eaten** an apple the day before.
'I **was eating** an apple.'	⟶ he **had been eating** an apple.
'I **have** already **eaten** it.'	⟶ he **had** already **eaten** it.
'I **have been eating** it for an hour.'	⟶ he **had been eating** it for an hour.
'I **had eaten** it before.'	⟶ he **had eaten** it before.

 2 Pronouns

When we want to put somebody else's words into indirect speech we change the pronouns **I**, **you** and **we**:

I ⟶ you, he, she
you ⟶ I, he, she, we
we ⟶ you, they

'**I**'m very tired today.' ⟶ He/she said (that) **he/she** was very tired that day.

'**You** look unhappy.' ⟶ She said (that) **I** looked unhappy.

'**We**'ve already been there.' ⟶ You said (that) **you**'d already been there.

 3 Modals

DIRECT SPEECH	INDIRECT SPEECH
can 'I **can** do it myself.'	⟶ **could** She said she **could** do it herself.
have to/must 'We **must** go.' 'We **have to** go.'	⟶ **had to** They said they **had to** go.
may 'You **may** leave early today.'	⟶ **might** The teacher said I **might** leave early.
shall 'I **shall** return on the twenty-second.'	⟶ **would** He said he **would** return on the twenty-second.
will 'I **will** send it tomorrow.'	⟶ **would** She said she **would** send it the next day.

The modals **could, might, ought to, should** and **would** do not change in indirect speech:

'I **might** go to the party later.' ⟶ She said she **might** go to the party later.

'I **would** prefer a cup of tea.' ⟶ He said he **would** prefer a cup of tea.

 4 Time (and some other) words

Time words are chosen in relation to the moment of speaking. They, and some other words, are changed in indirect speech so that the logic of the original words is retained.

DIRECT SPEECH		INDIRECT SPEECH
here	⟶	there
now	⟶	then, at that time
at the moment	⟶	at that moment
today	⟶	(on) that day
yesterday	⟶	the day before, the previous day
tomorrow	⟶	the next day, the following day
ago	⟶	before
this	⟶	that
these	⟶	those

'**At the moment** I have no money.' ⟶ She said (that) **at that moment** she had no money.

'We moved **here** two years **ago**.' ⟶ She said (that) they had moved there two years **before**.

 ## 5 Questions

There are two question systems in direct speech, one with QUESTION WORDS (see Chapter 5), one without:

A DIRECT SPEECH		INDIRECT SPEECH
'**Do** you **speak** Chinese?'	⟶	He asked **if*** I **spoke** Chinese.
'**Does** he **live** here?'	⟶	She asked **if** he **lived** there.
'**Have** you **seen** that film?'	⟶	He asked **if** we **had seen** that film.
		*****whether** can be used instead of **if**.

B DIRECT SPEECH		INDIRECT SPEECH
'**When did** you **arrive**?'	⟶	He asked **when** you **had arrived**.
'**Where do** you **live**?'	⟶	She asked **where** they **lived**.
'**How long has** he **been** here?'	⟶	I asked **how long** he **had been** there.

| PAST TIME | NOW |

Notice that in reported questions, after the question words **when**, **where**, etc. the word order is that of a statement and *not* a question:

He asked me where **I was** studying.
not
He asked me where **was I** studying.

 Questions which request suggestions or advice (often containing the modals **can**, **shall** or **should**) can be reported in two ways:

DIRECT SPEECH	INDIRECT SPEECH (1)	INDIRECT SPEECH (2)
'Where **shall I** go?'	She asked me **where to** go.	She asked me **where she should** go.
'What **should I** say?'	He asked me **what to** say.	He asked me **what he should** say.
'How **can I** tell him?'	She asked me **how to** tell him.	She asked me **how she could** tell him.
but 'How **do** I use this?'	He asked me how to use it.	—

See also QUESTION WORD + **to** + INFINITIVE (13.3).

6 Imperatives

> EMPLOYER: Now I want all you new workers to
> understand the rules here. We run an orderly factory
> and we don't want you to spoil it. Here are the rules.
> Don't forget to clock in in the morning! Always take
> your tea-break at the same time – that is, at ten o'clock.
> Don't try to walk out of the building with any tools or
> anything that belongs to the factory. And remember!
> Don't forget to switch off the electricity to all the
> machines . . .
>
> LAZY JIM (*who has just arrived and missed the
> instructions*): Arthur. I missed all that. What did the
> boss say?
>
> ARTHUR: He said that he wanted us to understand all the
> rules. He **told us not to forget** to clock in. He **said we
> should take** our tea-breaks at ten o'clock every
> morning. And he **warned us not to try** to walk out of
> the building with any tools. Finally he **said that we
> shouldn't forget** to switch off the machines. It's a good
> start, isn't it?

told us not to forget
said we should take
warned us not to try
said that we
shouldn't forget

 USE

When somebody gives an order or command we can put it into
indirect speech in the following two ways:

1 with **to** + INFINITIVE (or NEGATIVE INFINITIVE).
2 with a clause beginning **should, ought to, must,** etc.

DIRECT SPEECH	INDIRECT SPEECH
'**Close** the door!'	↗ He told me **to close** the door. *or* ↘ He said (that) I **should** close the door.
'**Switch** the machine off!'	↗ He told me **to switch** the machine off. *or* ↘ He said (that) I **should** switch the machine off.
'**Don't speak** to me!'	↗ He told me **not to speak** to him. *or* ↘ He said (that) I **shouldn't** speak to him.

When we want to convey the urgency of an order we can introduce the reported version with a verb other than **say** or **tell**:

'Get out of bed immediately!' ⟶ She **ordered** him to get out of bed immediately.

'Don't touch the wire! You'll get a shock.' ⟶ I **warned** him not to touch the wire because he would get a shock.

What did the policeman say?

He **said** that Paul **shouldn't** touch the wire.

He **warned** Paul **not to touch** the wire.

20.4 Bird's eye box: Indirect (reported) speech

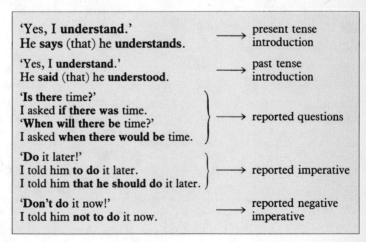

'Yes, I **understand**.' He **says** (that) he **understands**.	⟶ present tense introduction
'Yes, I **understand**.' He **said** (that) he **understood**.	⟶ past tense introduction
'**Is there** time?' I asked **if there was** time. '**When will there be** time?' I asked **when there would be** time.	⟶ reported questions
'**Do** it later!' I told him **to do** it later. I told him **that he should do** it later.	⟶ reported imperative
'**Don't do** it now!' I told him **not to do** it now.	⟶ reported negative imperative

21 PREPOSITIONS

21.1 Prepositions of place

in, near
at, on

from

along
to, through
on
towards
on
in
round
in front of

JOHN: We're having the meeting **in** a hotel **near** London. Actually, it will be **at** the village of Seaford. It's **on** the coast.

PETER: I'm afraid you'll have to describe the way **from** Colchester.

JOHN: Right. You drive **along** the motorway till you get **to** the North Circular Road. Then you go **through** London. I'll write the road number **on** a piece of paper. And then you simply drive **towards** Seaford. It's marked **on** the signposts.

PETER: Where do I go when I'm **in** the village?

JOHN: Drive **round** the village until you find the church. Just there, **in front of** it, you'll see the hotel.

––––––––– **form** –––––––––

preposition + noun

above   the house

The big cloud is **above** the house.

across the table

trees **along** the road

among(**st**) the people

(a)round the corner

at the bus-stop

behind the bus

below the window

beneath the bridge

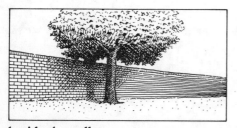

beside the **wall**

between Paul and Sally

by a river

from the shop

in front of the house

off the bus

on the sea

on to a bicycle

(he can look) **over** the mountains

through a telescope

to the bank

towards a policeman

under the table

Position – where

We use PREPOSITIONS OF PLACE to say **where** something or somebody is in relation to something else. Look at the house below:

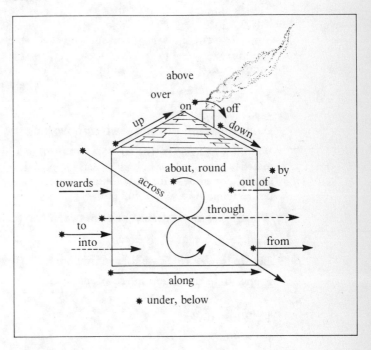

The plane is flying **above** (**over**) the city.

We were sitting **on** very comfortable seats.

Our house is **next to** the park.

I found it **behind** the wardrobe.

21.2 Prepositions of time

for	CHRIS: I've been working in Rome **for** three months now and I must say I really like it.
since	JANE: You've been living here **since** April, haven't you?
from, to, on	CHRIS: Yes. But the problem is that my contract only lasts **from** April **to** September. In fact, **on** September 1st I should really leave.
until	JANE: Well, you can enjoy yourself **until** September at least. And do you know what you can do? Wait a while
in	and then **in** July you can apply for another job. There
by	should be plenty of jobs available **by** then.

217

───────────── **form** ─────────────

preposition	+ noun or adverb	preposition	+ noun or adverb
after	breakfast	from	Thursday
at	Christmas	to	Monday
before	lunch-time	in	November
between	five o'clock	on	3rd April
	and six o'clock	throughout	the day
by	tomorrow	till	next week
during	the concert	until	Wednesday
		within	an hour

USE

Point/duration of time – when/how long

We put a PREPOSITION OF TIME in front of a noun or adverb in order to describe **when** an action happened, happens or will happen, or to describe **how long** an action lasted, lasts or will last in relation to something else:

We ate cheese and drank coffee **between** twelve and two.

We have lunch **at** twelve o'clock.

Before three o'clock we'll have time for a short walk.

Prepositions describe time relationships.

1   The clock

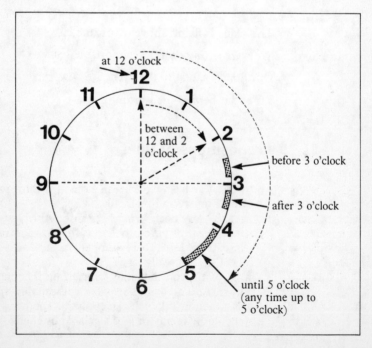

218

PREPOSITION	MEANING	OFTEN USED WITH*	
after	→ later than	→ points in time	→ **after** 2.30
at	→ talks about a point in time	→ time on the clock	→ **at** four o'clock
before	→ earlier than	→ points in time	→ **before** six o'clock
by	→ not later than	→ points in time	→ **by** 1999
between	→ the period **from** one point in time **to** another	→ two points in time	→ **between** 2 and 3.30 **between** Tuesday and Friday
during	→ continuing through a period	→ periods of time	→ **during** the night
in	→ in the course of, within a period of	→ months years	→ **in** February → **in** 1985
on	→ at the time of	→ dates days	→ **on** February 2nd → **on** Monday
throughout	→ right through, from end to end	→ periods of time	→ **throughout** the night
until (till)	→ to the time when, up to	→ points in time, complete events	→ **until** 9.30 **until** the evening
within	→ inside a period of time – not more than	→ periods of time	→ **within** six months

*This list does not cover *all* uses.

21.3 Other prepositions and prepositional phrases

in spite of	GERHARD: We had a great barbecue yesterday, **in spite of** the weather. STEPHEN: Where did you hold it?
against with except	GERHARD: On the beach! I know it's really **against** the rules but we lit a fire **with** some old wood and we were really careful. We all helped with the cooking, **except** Louis and he was in charge of the wine! STEPHEN: Sounds like I missed a good party.
according to	GERHARD: **According to** the others it was the best party ever!

───── **form** ─────

preposition/prep. phrase + noun

	according to	the policeman
against		the law
	apart from	the soldier
besides		his money
(made)by		the carpenter
despite		the weather
except		the soldier
	in spite of	the weather
(made)of		wood
with		the glasses
without		any money

PREPOSITIONS

 **Meanings**

PREPOSITION/ PREPOSITIONAL PHRASE	EXAMPLE	MEANING
according to	⟶ **According to** him you must pay £5.	⟶ In his opinion you must pay £5.
against	⟶ Nottingham Forest played **against** Liverpool.	⟶ Nottingham Forest played in opposition to Liverpool.
besides	⟶ **Besides** Jenny and Bob, who will be at the party?	⟶ In addition to Jenny and Bob, who will be at the party?
by	⟶ The old paintings were bought **by** Mr Clooney. (see PASSIVE, 17.3)	⟶ Mr Clooney bought the old paintings.
despite in spite of	⟶ **Despite** the bad weather we went swimming. (**In spite of** the bad weather . . .)	⟶ Though the weather was bad, we went swimming.
except apart from	⟶ There was nobody there **except** the teacher. (. . . **apart from** the teacher.)	⟶ The teacher was the only one there.
of	⟶ The boat is made **of** wood.	⟶ The material the boat is made from is wood. It is a wooden boat.
with (1)	⟶ She wrote **with** a black pen.	⟶ She used a black pen in order to write.
with (2)	⟶ He came **with** his sister.	⟶ He came in the company of his sister.
without	⟶ She decided to go **without** a coat.	⟶ She decided to go but not to take a coat.

21.4 Verbs plus prepositions

talk about

worry about

look at

believes in

think of

escaping from

live on, get bored
with, moan about

> JILL: Money! That's all people seem to **talk about**
> nowadays. You'd think they didn't have anything else
> to **worry about**.
> PENNY: Well, I think you should **look at** the facts.
> Everything is more expensive. There's inflation.
> Nobody **believes in** the government.
> JILL: Yes! Sometimes I **think of** forgetting everything
> and **escaping from** the world to a desert island.
> PENNY: That's not very realistic! What kind of food
> would you **live on**? Anyway, you'd probably **get bored
> with** having nothing to **moan about**!

form

verb	+ preposition	verb	+ preposition
agree	on	hope	for
believe	in	part	with
consist	of	shout	at
differ	from	think	about

USE

Verbs with particular prepositions

Some verbs are often used with particular prepositions. These
prepositions stand immediately after the verb. They do not
change the meaning of the verb:

Pauline is **asking for** a pizza.
——→ Pauline is ordering a pizza.
Terry **suffered from** stomach trouble for a long time.
People seem to want to **compete with** each other all the time.
Why are you **laughing at** me?
I'm really not **used to** such cold weather.

21.5 Bird's eye box: Prepositions

He lives **in** a tower block.	——→ preposition of place
We'll meet **at** seven o'clock.	——→ preposition of time
Robbery is **against** the law.	——→ prepositions/prepositional phrases
The referee **shouted at** the footballers.	——→ verb plus preposition

22 PHRASAL VERBS

CONTENTS		page
22.1	Phrasal verbs (general)	222
22.1.1	Two particles: adverb + preposition	223
22.2	Bird's eye box (phrasal verbs)	224

22.1 Phrasal verbs (general)

drop in on
looking forward to

get on with

fit in with

> JOHN: Hi, Sarah. How are you?
> SARAH: Hello. This is a coincidence. I was just going to **drop in on** you. I was **looking forward to** a cup of your coffee!
> JOHN: I'm just going to see some friends down the road. Why don't you come too? I'm sure you'll **get on with** them.
> SARAH: I'll **fit in with** whatever you want to do – it's just good to see you again.

────────── **form** ──────────

verb + particle(s)

hold	out
let	down
look	forward to
drop	in on (someone)
get	on with (someone)

USE

Special verb phrases

We use a verb and a particle (either an adverb or a preposition) to create a verb phrase, called a PHRASAL VERB, with a new meaning:

VERB ⟶ MEANING	⟶ PHRASAL VERB (VERB + PARTICLE)	⟶ MEANING
let ⟶ allow, give permission	⟶ **let down**	⟶ disappoint
turn ⟶ move something around	⟶ **turn down**	⟶ reject, say 'no' to

Word order

When we have a NOUN (see Chapter 2) as object after the verb we
can change the position of the particle: it can go before or after
the object, without changing the meaning:

object noun before particle	object noun after particle(s)
The police set **the trap** up. ⟶	The police set up **the trap**.

When the object of the verb is a PRONOUN (see Chapter 4),
the first order is the more usual (the object before the
particle). The second order is used when there are two particles
or when the particle is a preposition:

object pronoun before particle	object pronoun after particle(s)
He put **the books** down. ↓ He put **them** down.	She takes after **her father**. ↓ She takes after **him**. They came up with **a good idea**. ↓ They came up with **it**.

22.1.1 Two particles: adverb + preposition

English has many three-part phrasal verbs. These consist of a
verb followed by two particles, the first an ADVERB (see
Chapter 7), the second a PREPOSITION (see Chapter 21):

be out of ⟶ She **was out of** sugar.
meaning
She had no sugar.

be up to ⟶ What **were** you **up to** last night?
meaning
What were you doing last night?

stand in for ⟶ Could you **stand in for** me at tomorrow's
meeting?
meaning
Could you take my place at tomorrow's
meeting?

When the object of a three-part phrasal verb is a pronoun it follows the particles:

She was out of sugar. ⟶ She was out of **it**.
He backed out of the agreement. ⟶ He backed out of **it**.

22.2 Bird's eye box: Phrasal verbs

The milk **went off**. ⟶	phrasal verb (one particle)
They turned **it** down. ⟶	pronoun object (usual word order)
I took **her** out. ⟶	pronoun object (preposition particle)
The car **ran out of** petrol. ⟶	two particles
I'd come to the party but I'm not up to **it**. ⟶	pronoun object (two particles)

23 LINKING WORDS

CONTENTS   *page*

23.1 Linking words (general)

Linking words are used to join two sentences or clauses and so show the relationship between them:

| 1 | 2 | | 1 | 2 |

He is big. He is strong.   He is small. He can run very fast.

He is big **and** strong.   He is small **but** he can run very fast.

You can **either** have the prize **or** take the money. (**positive**)
⟶ You can do only one of these.

She can **neither** ride a bicycle **nor** drive a car. (**negative**)
⟶ She does not know how to ride a bicycle. She does not know how to drive a car.

23.2 Time linking words

now that

before

when

as soon as

Now that I have finished my university studies I hope to become a teacher.

   I studied literature for three years **before** taking a teacher training course. In England you can start university **when** you have completed your A-level examinations at school. I started university **as soon as** I left school, but many young people prefer to take a year off so that they can get some work experience.

---

form

clause	+ linking word(s) +	clause
I went shopping	before	I came home.
She did some work	after	he had left the house.
He felt happier	as soon as	they had paid the money.
He's easier to work with	once	you begin to believe in him.
She remembered being nervous	when	he was a soldier.
They stay inside	whenever	it rains.
The committee left	while	the president was speaking.

---

 1 Clauses

LINKING WORDS often introduce a SUBORDINATE CLAUSE (4.12 ☞ 2). This is an extra sentence which is added to a MAIN CLAUSE (4.12 ☞ 2). The meaning of the subordinate clause is dependent on the main clause:

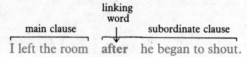

A clause normally has its own subject and verb:

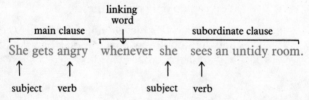

USE

Saying when or how long

We use TIME LINKING WORDS to introduce TIME CLAUSES. These give information about *when* something happens or *for how long* it continues:

I cleaned the car (⟶ **when?** ⟶) just **before** it rained.

Paul has to wait (⟶ **how long?** ⟶) **until** the others arrive.

2 Details of time linking words

LINKING WORD(S)	MEANING	EXAMPLE
after	→ at a later time than	→ **After** I had visited Greece I began to learn Greek.
as	→ at the moment when	→ It fell over **as** he climbed into the boat.
as soon as	→ the moment after	→ **As soon as** he left the room the pupils began to shout.
before	→ at an earlier time than	→ I had fetched the menu **before** the waiter arrived at the table.
once	→ when → as soon as	→ **Once** you have learned to swim you never forget.
since	→ from that point of time to now	→ We have known each other **since** we were children.
until (till)	→ up to the time when	→ You must wait **until** you are twenty-one years old.
when	→ at the time	→ **When** you leave the room switch the lights out.
whenever	→ every time that	→ **Whenever** I see pistols and knives I get nervous.
while	→ at the same time as	→ **While** Peter was driving to Scotland he had an accident.

23.2.1 Future time clauses

| after | as | as soon as | before |
| once | until (till) | when | whenever | while |

When these linking words are used to talk about a future action, they are followed by a PRESENT TENSE (11.1–11.6), not a FUTURE TENSE (11.26–11.34):

As soon as he **pays** the bill, we will go.
⟶ present simple (*not* **will pay**)

I'm going to wait **until** she's **sleeping**.
⟶ present continuous (*not* **will sleep**)

See also CONDITIONAL SENTENCES (19.1).

23.3 Reason linking words

that's why	JOHN: I always wanted to be a racing driver. **That's why** I used to go to the racing circuit to practise. I couldn't
because	go very often **because** I just didn't have enough money. I was fifteen years old and although my parents wanted me to be a teacher I was only interested in fast cars.
that was the reason why because	**That was the reason why** I didn't take a part-time job to get extra money. I just went to the training circuit **because** I wanted to be a part of the atmosphere.

────────────── **form** ──────────────

clause	+ linking word(s)	+ clause
I couldn't go abroad	as	I didn't have enough money.
He left	because	he wanted to get home early.
She wasn't upset	since	she didn't really want to go.
We had to go to hospital.	That's why	we weren't able to come.
They were robbed.	That's the reason why	they couldn't pay on time.

USE

Saying why

We use REASON LINKING WORDS to give information about **why** something happens:

'Why did you buy a new colour television?'
'I bought it **because** my old one kept breaking down.'

'Why didn't you come to our appointment?'
'**Because of** the weather.'

'Why can't you pay me the £5 you owe me?'
'**Since** my pay cheque isn't paid until tomorrow, I can't give you the money until then.'

'**As** I live in a flat I don't know much about gardening.'

Because, **since**, **that's why** and **as** all have similar meanings and usages.

23.4 Result linking words

so . . . that	TERRY: the train was **so** late this morning **that** I missed my connection in Glasgow.
	PAT: What did you do about it? You had an important meeting in Newcastle, didn't you?
as a result	TERRY: Yes, and I had to get there on time. Well, I missed my connection and **as a result** I was going to be
so	three hours late. **So** I had to think of something. I phoned for a taxi and drove to Edinburgh.
consequently	**Consequently** I was able to get a connection to Newcastle from there.

form

clause	+ linking word(s)	+ clause
We were frightened.	As a result	we decided to go to the police.
The window was open.	Consequently As a consequence	the thief escaped.
Peter stayed there	so (that)	I was obliged to go home by myself.
His condition was	such that	we had to call a doctor.
There were no supporters.	Therefore	the team lost the match.

USE	**Describing results/consequences**

We use RESULT LINKING WORDS when we want to describe the result or consequence of a situation:

It rained **so** much **that** the river overflowed its banks.

the result was

My friend didn't arrive for our appointment **so**
I went to the cinema without him.

the result was

Result linking words all mean 'as a result'.

They can all be used in a similar way, but **consequently** is more formal than the others:

I broke my leg **so** I had to go to hospital.

He ate so much ice-cream **that** he felt sick.

She ate **such** a lot of ice-cream **that** she felt sick.

He spent a great deal of money and **consequently** is overdrawn at the bank.

23.5 Contrast linking words

but	PETE: Where do you want to go on holiday this year? I fancy the Canary Islands. ANN: Oh no! I can't. I'd like to, **but** I can't stand flying. I get ill. PETE: OK. We could still go somewhere in the south,
although on the other hand	**although** it probably won't be as warm. ANN: Well, **on the other hand** we could drive down to Yugoslavia or Greece in the camping bus.
even though	PETE: **Even though** I like driving, I'm not sure I want to drive that far! Haven't you got any other ideas!

form

clause	+ linking word(s)	+ clause
We'd like you to stand by	although	we believe we can still manage the situation.
They wanted to stay longer	but	they simply didn't have the time.

clause	+ linking word(s)	+ clause
We knew what they'd done	even though	they never told us the truth.
I don't think we'll succeed.	However,	we should at least try.
She'd be good company.	On the other hand	she doesn't have any money.
I listened to his story	though	I never believed it.
She likes to drink coffee	whereas while*	he prefers to drink tea.

*See also TIME LINKING WORDS (23.2–23.2.1).

USE

Contrasting two pieces of information

We use CONTRAST LINKING WORDS when we want to relate two facts which seem at variance with (or in contrast to) each other:

first fact   second fact

I don't think we can succeed, **although** we can try if you want.

first fact   second fact

They drink coffee every morning, **whereas** we drink tea.

Details of contrast linking words

LINKING WORD(S)	MEANING	EXAMPLE
however **but**	→ nevertheless →	I can't come to London on Saturday. **However,** I can come the Saturday after. She wanted to be at work on time **but** she couldn't start her car.
on the other hand →	the other consideration is →	I'd like to work to earn some money. **On the other hand** I should finish university.

LINKING WORD(S)	MEANING	EXAMPLE
although/ though	→ in spite of the fact that	→ She didn't give me the money back **though** she said she would.
even though	→ like **though** but stronger. Used to call attention to something of an extreme nature.	→ He jumped into the water to help **even though** he couldn't swim.
whereas **while**	→ in contrast with the fact that	Jane prefers to go dancing **whereas** Jill likes swimming. He likes skiing **while** she enjoys windsurfing.

23.6 Purpose linking words

in order to

to
so that

to

TOMMY: Last year I visited Greece **in order to** get some idea of the food and the people.
SAMMY: And what impressions did you get?
TOMMY: Well, I liked it so much that I came back to England last winter **to** get a qualification in Teaching English as a Foreign Language **so that** I could work in Greece for a couple of years.
SAMMY: So you're only here to pass the exam and then you're going off again.
TOMMY: That's it. In fact, I only came to see you **to** say goodbye. I'm leaving for Athens next week.

form

clause	+ linking word(s)	+ clause
I'll catch the early train	so as to	be there in time.
We took our credit cards	so that	we would be able to pay.
Listen carefully	in order that	you understand the rules.
You'll have to practise	in order to	pass the driving test.
She took classes	to	improve her English.

USE

Giving reasons

We use PURPOSE LINKING WORDS to introduce the reason(s) for an action. They all have a similar meaning and are used in a similar way, apart from **so as to** and **in order to** which are more formal:

The police stopped the car **in order to** check the brakes.

She telephoned **so that** she could give him the news.

The government passed the bill **so as to** increase their revenue.

He went to the Indonesian restaurant **to*** try different food.

*Very common usage. See **to** + INFINITIVE (PURPOSE) (13.4).

23.7 Comparison linking words

than	JOHN: How do you like this new café? It's rather good, isn't it?
not . . . as . . . as	CYNTHIA: Well, I admit the coffee tastes much better **than** the coffee in some of the cafés here in Canterbury. But it's **not** quite as good as Torino's in London.
not as . . . as	JOHN: That may be, but it's **not as** expensive **as** it is in London, either.
as . . . as	CYNTHIA: Anyone who drinks coffee **as** much **as** you do must be an expert. Have you ever thought of writing a book called *Places to drink good coffee in England*?

form

LINKING WORDS	EXAMPLE
as . . . as	⟶ He was **as** strong **as** an ox.
(not) as . . . as	⟶ She is **(not) as** hard-working **as** her brother (is).
not so . . . as	⟶ She is **not so** hard-working **as** her brother (is).
. . . than	⟶ They paid more money for their house **than** we did.

USE

Comparing things or people

We use COMPARISON LINKING WORDS when we are comparing two people, situations or things:

Your dog is more aggressive **than** ours (is).
The petrol here isn't **as** expensive **as** the petrol in Italy (is).
⟶ Petrol costs more in Italy.

See COMPARATIVE ADJECTIVES (6.5–6.5.1) for details, and also CONDITIONAL LINKING WORDS (19.1 ☞ 1).

23.8 Bird's eye box: Linking words

He had read the book **before** he saw the film.	⟶ time
I'll give you the ticket **when** you **give** me the money.	⟶ future time, present tense
She left **because** she was angry.	⟶ reason
We had no more money **so** we had to come home.	⟶ result
Although she came by car, she still arrived late.	⟶ contrast
I went on a diet **so that** I could lose weight.	⟶ purpose
He's **as** brave **as** a lion.	⟶ comparison

24 PUNCTUATION

CONTENTS

24.1 Punctuation (general)

capital letter
comma
full stop
dash
hyphen

quotation marks

exclamation mark
question mark
brackets

apostrophe

(I)t was a cold, rainy morning. I walked down the road of one of the many back streets in this depressing(,) industrial, Victorian city(.) The first thing to do was to get some cash from the bank (–) a thing I always had to do on Monday morning. The week (-) ends were expensive. I walked into the bank. It was unusually quiet. Suddenly a voice shouted, (")Get over here. Put your hands up.(")

"My God(!)" I thought to myself, "I'm in the middle of a bank robbery. What am I going to do(?)"

The question was answered for me ((though not as I had expected()). I felt a pain at the back of my head. My last thought was – "I(')m going to die." After that I remember nothing.

form		
mark		name
A B C etc.	$\longrightarrow$	capital letters
. . . .	$\longrightarrow$	full stop
. . . , . . .	$\longrightarrow$	comma
. . . : . . .	$\longrightarrow$	colon
. . . ; . . .	$\longrightarrow$	semicolon
. . . - . . .	$\longrightarrow$	dash
(. . .)	$\longrightarrow$	brackets
[. . .]	$\longrightarrow$	square brackets
. . . ?	$\longrightarrow$	question mark
. . . !	$\longrightarrow$	exclamation mark
. . . ' . . .	$\longrightarrow$	apostrophe
. . . - . . .	$\longrightarrow$	hyphen
" . . . "	$\longrightarrow$	quotation marks/inverted
' . . . '		commas

USE

Clarification of meaning

We use punctuation marks to make it easier for a reader to understand what we mean. They clarify the intended sense of a passage.

24.2 Capital Letters

1 We use a capital letter *to start a sentence*

It cost the company more than £10,000. The main problem was that this company had borrowed too much money from the bank.

2 When a person talks about him- or herself he or she uses **I**. The personal pronoun (subject) **I** is always a capital letter:

David did not realize that **I** had already paid the bill.

3 We use a capital letter *at the beginning of a proper noun*. Proper nouns are *names*. We put a capital letter at the beginning of:

236

geographical names	⟶	cities countries islands
		seas mountains lakes
		streets roads

all other names	⟶	people nationalities races
		titles religions festivals

I think that **M**adrid is the capital of **S**pain.

The **R**ocky **M**ountains have always attracted a certain type of tourist.

Christmas is a **C**hristian celebration.

24.3 Full stop . . . .

1 We put a full stop *at the end of a sentence* to show that it has finished:

> David says that they argue about almost everything(.)
> You ought to go on a diet before it's too late(.)

2 We put a full stop *after words which we have shortened* (abbreviated):

> Prof(.)Marcus Wheeler wrote the *Oxford Russian Dictionary*.
> ⟶ Professor Marcus Wheeler wrote the *Oxford Russian Dictionary*.
> That's Rev(.)Wilson. He's our local vicar.
> ⟶ That's Reverend Wilson. He's our local vicar.

3 We put a full stop *after an abbreviation* which is a *single letter*:

> That's the Right Honourable S. Treacher, M(.)P(.)
> ⟶ That's . . . Treacher, Member of Parliament.

24.4 Comma . . . , . . .

1 We use commas *to separate individual items in lists*. The words may be nouns, adjectives, adverbs or verbs.

> Could you get me the following things from the shop: a loaf of bread(,)some potatoes(,)a cabbage and some cooking oil.

> The tall(,) handsome and rather shy boy asked her to dance.

We do not normally put a comma before **and** in such a list.

2 We can use a comma *to divide off a subsidiary phrase or clause from the main sentence*. The phrase or clause can be lifted out of the main sentence without changing its meaning:

The flat(,)which was really very expensive(,)has been sold already.
Sons and Lovers(,)written by D. H. Lawrence(,)is one of the most important novels of the twentieth century.

3 We put a comma *after certain words which introduce a sentence*:

Well(,)I don't necessarily agree with what you say.

MRS BLACK: Did I see you at the cinema yesterday evening?
MRS PEACH: No(,)I was at a meeting last night.

24.5 Colon ...:...

1 We use a colon *to introduce a list of items or articles:*

First, buy the ingredients of a pizza(:)tomatoes, cheese, salami and pizza bread.

2 We use a colon *to indicate we are going to give more detail* about a point made:

Maureen and her sister Margaret are very different(:) Maureen's tall, slim, pretty and stupid while Margaret's short, plump, plain and very intelligent.

24.6 Semicolon ...;...

A semicolon may be used (instead of the more usual full stop) to mark the completion of a topic before continuing with a related topic, or (instead of the more usual comma) between items in a list. It makes a shorter pause than a full stop, but a longer pause than a comma:

Mozart wrote beautiful music(;)da Ponte wrote the libretti for some of his best operas.
Cambridge University is composed of many colleges: King's(;) Trinity(;)Emmanuel are a few of them.

24.7 Dash ...−...

We can use dashes *to divide off a phrase or word from the main sentence*, although it is considered better to use COMMAS (24.4):

Kathryn(−)the youngest daughter(−)has just got a job in a bank.

24.8 Brackets (. . .)

1 When we want *to add extra information* which is not vitally important, we can put it between brackets. There is little difference between two dashes and brackets:

EXAMINER: I want you to begin to write in your answer books (they are on the desks in front of you) when I give you the signal.

2 We put brackets *round dates* showing when a person was born and died:

John S. Smith (1840–84) was one of the best-known architects in the city of York.

24.9 Question mark . . . ?

We put a question mark *at the end of a question*:

'What time do you think the train will arrive(?)' he asked.
When did you last see a really good film(?)

If the question sentence is, in fact, a command or request and not a true question we can leave the question mark out:

Could you open the window, please.

24.10 Exclamation mark . . . !

We use an exclamation mark *after direct speech exclamations and commands*:

'He found £1,000 in the street(!)'
'No(!)How extraordinary(!)'
'Be careful(!)'
'Be quiet(!)'
'Quickly, close the window(!)'

24.11 Apostrophe . . . ' . . .

1 We use an apostrophe *to show that a letter/letters or number/numbers is missing*:

('63 $\longrightarrow$ 1963 (1863, 1763, etc.)
I was born in ('49. $\longrightarrow$ in 1949
I('m $\longrightarrow$ I am
he('s $\longrightarrow$ he is
we('re $\longrightarrow$ we are
doesn('t $\longrightarrow$ does not

2 We also use an apostrophe *to show that somebody is the owner of something* (see NOUNS AND POSSESSION (2.4)):

Jennifer Ⓘs friend   ⟶ the friend of Jennifer
Mr Smith Ⓘs motor car ⟶ the motor car of Mr Smith

When the owner is more than one person, the apostrophe comes after the **s**:

The teachers Ⓘroom   ⟶ the room of the teachers
The secretaries Ⓘduties ⟶ the duties of the
                                        secretar**ies**

24.12 Hyphen . . . - . . .

1 We can use a hyphen *with certain prefixes*:

ex- self- all- pseudo- mini- mid- trans-
⟶ ex-employee mid-August self-respect

2 It is also used *to link two or more words which are used together* so often they are thought of as a single word:

twenty-three mother-in-law well-known ice-cube

24.13 Quotation marks " . . . "/' . . .'

1 We use quotation marks *to mark off direct speech*:

Mark shouted, ⒾLook out! There's something behind you. Ⓘ

2 Quotation marks are also used *to indicate another person's words when they are quoted exactly*; these may come from a play, film, book or actual speech:

Or, as Shakespeare observed, ⒾLife's but a walking shadow, a poor player that struts and frets his hour upon the stage, and then is heard no more. Ⓘ

Either single or double quotation marks can be used.

24.14 Bird's eye box: Punctuation

A B C etc.	⟶ capital letter	⟶ at the beginning of a sentence
		⟶ personal pronoun (subject) **I**
		⟶ proper nouns (names)
. . . .	⟶ full stop	⟶ at the end of a sentence
		⟶ after abbreviations
. . . ,	⟶ comma	⟶ between items in a list
		⟶ to divide off clauses/phrases
		⟶ after introductory words
. . . :	⟶ colon	⟶ to introduce lists
		⟶ to introduce detail
. . . ;	⟶ semicolon	⟶ between items in a list or between related topics in a sentence
. . . – . . .	⟶ dash	⟶ to divide off words/phrases
(. . .)	⟶ brackets	⟶ round extra information
		⟶ round birth and death dates
. . . ?	⟶ question mark	⟶ at the end of questions
. . . !	⟶ exclamation mark	⟶ after exclamations/commands
. . . ' . . .	⟶ apostrophe	⟶ to indicate missing letter(s)/number(s)
		⟶ to show possession
. . . - . . .	⟶ hyphen	⟶ with some prefixes
		⟶ in compound words
" . . . "/ ' . . . '	⟶ quotation marks	⟶ marking off direct speech and to quote

APPENDIX– IRREGULAR VERBS

Verbs marked * also have a regular form. See the list at the end of this section.

INFINITIVE	PAST SIMPLE	PAST PARTICIPLE (for PRESENT PERFECT, PAST PERFECT, FUTURE PERFECT and PASSIVE)
arise	arose	arisen
awake	awoke	awoken
be	was/were	been
beat	beat	beat
become	became	become
begin	began	begun
bend	bent	bent
*bet	bet	bet
bid	bid	bid
bind	bound	bound
bite	bit	bitten
bleed	bled	bled
blow	blew	blown
break	broke	broken
breed	bred	bred
bring	brought	brought
broadcast	broadcast	broadcast
build	built	built
*burn	burnt	burnt
burst	burst	burst
buy	bought	bought
cast	cast	cast
catch	caught	caught
choose	chose	chosen
cling	clung	clung
come	came	come
cost	cost	cost
creep	crept	crept
cut	cut	cut
deal	dealt	dealt
dig	dug	dug
do	did	done
draw	drew	drawn
*dream	dreamt	dreamt
drink	drank	drunk
drive	drove	driven
eat	ate	eaten
fall	fell	fallen
feed	fed	fed
feel	felt	felt
fight	fought	fought
find	found	found
fling	flung	flung

242

INFINITIVE	PAST SIMPLE	PAST PARTICIPLE (for PRESENT PERFECT, PAST PERFECT, FUTURE PERFECT and PASSIVE)
fly	flew	flown
forbid	forbade/forbad	forbidden
forecast	forecast	forecast
forget	forgot	forgotten
forgive	forgave	forgiven
freeze	froze	frozen
get	got	got
give	gave	given
go	went	gone (been)
grind	ground	ground
grow	grew	grown
*hang	hung	hung
have	had	had
hear	heard	heard
hide	hid	hidden
hit	hit	hit
hold	held	held
hurt	hurt	hurt
keep	kept	kept
*kneel	knelt	knelt
*knit	knit	knit
know	knew	known
lay	laid	laid
lead	led	led
*lean	leant	leant
*leap	leapt	leapt
*learn	learnt	learnt
leave	left	left
lend	lent	lent
let	let	let
lie	lay	lain
*light	lit	lit
lose	lost	lost
make	made	made
mean	meant	meant
meet	met	met
mistake	mistook	mistaken
misunderstand	misunderstood	misunderstood
mow	mowed	mown
overcome	overcame	overcome
pay	paid	paid
put	put	put
*quit	quit	quit
read	read	read
rid	rid	rid
ride	rode	ridden
ring	rang	rung
rise	rose	risen
run	ran	run
saw	sawed	sawn

APPENDIX – IRREGULAR VERBS

INFINITIVE	PAST SIMPLE	PAST PARTICIPLE (for PRESENT PERFECT, PAST PERFECT, FUTURE PERFECT and PASSIVE)
say	said	said
see	saw	seen
seek	sought	sought
sell	sold	sold
send	sent	sent
set	set	set
sew	sewed	sewn
shake	shook	shaken
shed	shed	shed
shine	shone	shone
shoot	shot	shot
show	showed	shown
shrink	shrank	shrunk
shut	shut	shut
sing	sang	sung
sink	sank	sunk
sit	sat	sat
sleep	slept	slept
slide	slid	slid
sling	slung	slung
slink	slunk	slunk
slit	slit	slit
*smell	smelt	smelt
sow	sowed	sown
speak	spoke	spoken
*speed	sped	sped
*spell	spelt	spelt
spend	spent	spent
*spill	spilt	spilt
spin	spun/span	spun
spit	spat	spat
split	split	split
*spoil	spoilt	spoilt
spread	spread	spread
spring	sprang	sprung
stand	stood	stood
steal	stole	stolen
stick	stuck	stuck
sting	stung	stung
stink	stank	stunk
stride	strode	stridden
strike	struck	struck
string	strung	strung
strive	strove	striven
swear	swore	sworn
*sweat	sweat	sweat
sweep	swept	swept
swell	swelled	swollen
swim	swam	swum
swing	swung	swung

244

INFINITIVE	PAST SIMPLE	PAST PARTICIPLE (for PRESENT PERFECT, PAST PERFECT, FUTURE PERFECT and PASSIVE)
take	took	taken
teach	taught	taught
tear	tore	torn
tell	told	told
think	thought	thought
throw	threw	thrown
thrust	thrust	thrust
tread	trod	trodden
understand	understood	understood
undertake	undertook	undertaken
upset	upset	upset
wake	woke	woken
wear	wore	worn
weave	wove	woven
weep	wept	wept
wet	wet	wet
win	won	won
wind	wound	wound
withdraw	withdrew	withdrawn
withhold	withheld	withheld
withstand	withstood	withstood
wring	wrung	wrung
write	wrote	written

Verbs marked * have an alternative regular form ending with **ed**. In the case of **hang**, the meaning changes:

He **hung** the picture on the wall.

⟶ He suspended the picture on the wall using a picture hook. (for *objects*)

They **hanged** him from a tree.

⟶ They killed him by putting a rope round his neck and hanging him from a tree. (for killing *animals* and *people*)

bet	betted	betted
burn	burned	burned
dream	dreamed	dreamed
hang	hanged	hanged
kneel	kneeled	kneeled
knit	knitted	knitted
lean	leaned	leaned
leap	leaped	leaped
learn	learned	learned
light	lighted	lighted
quit	quitted	quitted
smell	smelled	smelled
speed	speeded	speeded
spell	spelled	spelled
spill	spilled	spilled
spoil	spoiled	spoiled
sweat	sweated	sweated

ACKNOWLEDGEMENTS

Very special thanks to:

Joy McKellen (Penguin Books), for your patience and enthusiasm; for steering the boat through rough waters and for an understanding of the problems of an author – thank you.

Uschi Altmann (Free University, Berlin), for your comments and suggestions offered from the vantage point of a foreign learner and teacher, and for your psychological support.

Norma Innes (Anglo World, Bournemouth), for your intensive efforts during the finishing stages of the manuscript, being instrumental in the checking and reformulating of many items before the manuscript could be considered 'finished'. As an experienced teacher of English as a Foreign Language your advice and additions were invaluable. I am most grateful.

Prof. M. Wheeler (Queen's University, Belfast), for your long-lasting support in all my misbegotten projects.

Vivian Cook (University of Essex), for your comments and advice in the initial phases of writing this grammar.

Mario Rinvoluccri and the staff and students of Pilgrims School, Canterbury, for your help.

Hermione Ieronymidis (Penguin Books), for cementing all that had gone before into a potentially useful tool. Thanks for your very supportive background noises.

All others, for your comments.

Thanks to the Penguin team for peaceful, professional support.

INDEX

*

think followed by PREPOSITION 21.4; by
FUTURE SIMPLE 11.27
third ORDINAL NUMBER 1.2; in dates 1.2;
VULGAR FRACTION 1.4
this DEMONSTRATIVE PRONOUN 4.9;
DEMONSTRATIVE ADJECTIVE 4.10; before
GERUND 15.1; change in INDIRECT SPEECH
20.3.4
this this year/week/morning/evening/ with
PRESENT PERFECT or PRESENT SIMPLE
11.17.1
those DEMONSTRATIVE PRONOUN 4.9;
DEMONSTRATIVE ADJECTIVE 4.10; in
INDIRECT SPEECH 20.3.4
though CONTRAST LINKING WORD 23.5
three CARDINAL NUMBER 1.1
through PREPOSITION 21.1; followed by
GERUND 15.3
throughout PREPOSITION of TIME 21.2;
ADVERB 7.3
till PREPOSITION of TIME 21.2; LINKING
WORD 23.2; (for FUTURE TIME CLAUSE)
23.2.1
time ABSTRACT NOUN 2.1, 3.4.2; it's high
time followed by UNREAL PAST
(SUBJUNCTIVE) 12.1; at that time in
INDIRECT SPEECH 20.3.4; at the same time
as with PAST CONTINUOUS 11.15.1
TIME dates for definite time (with ORDINAL
NUMBERS) 1.2; how long? with PRESENT
PERFECT for QUESTIONS about 11.17;
when? for QUESTIONS about 5.1
DEMONSTRATIVE PRONOUNS to show
distance of 4.9
ADVERBS and ADVERBIAL PHRASES of 7.1,
7.2
PAST SIMPLE for periods of 11.11.1
PAST CONTINUOUS for events over a period
of 11.15.1–2
for for lengths of time, since for points of
time 11.17.2; expressed by PRESENT
PERFECT CONTINUOUS 11.19; will
expressing definite FUTURE 11.27; FUTURE
CONTINUOUS for two actions 11.29; FUTURE
PERFECT for actions completed by a certain
time 11.30
FUTURE PERFECT CONTINUOUS for actions
completed by a certain time 11.31
CHANGES in time words in INDIRECT
SPEECH 20.3.4; PREPOSITIONS of TIME
21.2; TIME LINKING WORDS 23.2, 23.2.1
times (three times, etc.) 1.3
tiring PRESENT PARTICIPLE as ADJECTIVE
16.1
to before OBJECT PRONOUN 4.1.2;
before RECIPROCAL PRONOUN 4.8;
before REFLEXIVE PRONOUN 4.15
to whom in FORMAL ENGLISH 4.12.3
to as part of MODAL VERB PHRASE: would
like to 10.6; would prefer to 10.6.1; ought to

10.9; have to 10.19; have got to 10.19; need
to 10.25; used to 10.27; dare to 10.29
from . . . to with PAST SIMPLE 11.11.1;
going to FUTURE 11.28; be to FUTURE 11.32
to + INFINITIVE Chapter 13; contrast with
GERUND 15.4, 15.5; in PASSIVE MODAL
VERB PHRASES 17.5; in PASSIVE
INFINITIVE 17.6; in INDIRECT QUESTIONS
20.3.5; in INDIRECT IMPERATIVES 20.3.6
PURPOSE LINKING WORD 23.6; PARTICLE
in PHRASAL VERB (e.g. look forward to)
22.1; PREPOSITION of PLACE/TIME 21.1,
21.2; PREPOSITION after VERB 21.4
today ADVERB of TIME 7.1; with PRESENT
PERFECT or PAST SIMPLE 11.17.1; changes
in INDIRECT SPEECH 20.3.4
tomorrow ADVERB of TIME 7.1; changes in
INDIRECT SPEECH 20.3.4
tone of voice in QUESTION TAGS 18.4
too plus ADJECTIVE followed by
to + INFINITIVE 13.2
tooth/teeth irregular PLURAL 2.3.1
towards 21.1
trans- 24.12
trousers NOUN only in PLURAL 2.3.2
true/truly IRREGULAR SPELLING of ADVERBS
of MANNER 7.4
try followed by to + INFINITIVE 13.5;
followed by GERUND or to + INFINITIVE
(different meaning) 15.5
two CARDINAL NUMBER 1.1
twice NUMBER of times 1.3

u see VOWELS; pronunciation after
INDEFINITE ARTICLE 3.6
UNCOUNTABLE NOUNS see NOUNS
under 21.1
under no circumstances ADVERB PHRASE of
RESTRICTION 7.5
understand STATIVE VERB 11.7; followed by
GERUND as OBJECT 15.2
unemployed 3.3
uniform 3.6
unique DEFINITE ARTICLE with something
unique 3.2
union 3.6
United Kingdom (the) 3.4.1
United States (the) 3.4.1
unless CONDITIONAL LINKING WORD; with
FIRST CONDITIONAL 19.1
up PREPOSITION 21.1; use in PHRASAL
VERBS 22.1, 22.1.1
UNREAL PAST see SUBJUNCTIVE
until PREPOSITION of TIME 21.2; LINKING
WORD used before CLAUSE 23.2.2
us PERSONAL PRONOUN (OBJECT)
4.1.1
use it's no use followed by GERUND 15.2
used to MODAL VERB: form 10.1; to express
past habit 10.27